Ground

by Lisa Dillman

A Samuel French Acting Edition

SAMUEL FRENCH

FOUNDED 1830

NEW YORK HOLLYWOOD LONDON TORONTO

SAMUELFRENCH.COM

ISBN 978-0-573-69902-3   Printed in U.S.A.   #29708

MUSIC USE NOTE

Licensees are solely responsible for obtaining formal written permission from copyright owners to use copyrighted music in the performance of this play and are strongly cautioned to do so. If no such permission is obtained by the licensee, then the licensee must use only original music that the licensee owns and controls. Licensees are solely responsible and liable for all music clearances and shall indemnify the copyright owners of the play and their licensing agent, Samuel French, Inc., against any costs, expenses, losses and liabilities arising from the use of music by licensees.

IMPORTANT BILLING AND CREDIT REQUIREMENTS

All producers of *GROUND* must give credit to the Author of the Play in all programs distributed in connection with performances of the Play, and in all instances in which the title of the Play appears for the purposes of advertising, publicizing or otherwise exploiting the Play and/or a production. The name of the Author *must* appear on a separate line on which no other name appears, immediately following the title and *must* appear in size of type not less than fifty percent of the size of the title type.

In addition the following credit *must* be given in all programs and publicity information distributed in association with this piece:

World premiere in the 2010 Humana Festival of New American Plays at Actors Theatre of Louisville.

Originally commissioned by Northlight Theatre, Skokie, Ill.
(BJ Jones, Artistic Director; Timothy J. Evans, Executive Director)

actors theatre of louisville

34th annual Humana Festival of New American Plays
made possible by a generous grant from The Humana Foundation

Ground

by **Lisa Dillman**
directed by **Marc Masterson**

THE CAST
(in order of appearance)

Carl Zelaya	**Dale Rivera***
Zelda Preston	**Jennifer Engstrom***
Angie (Ochoa) Zelaya	**Sandra Delgado***
Cooper Daniels	**Rob Riley***
Chuy Gallegos	**Ricardo Gutierrez***
Ines (Ochoa) Sandoval	**Liza Fernandez***

Originally commissioned by Northlight Theatre, Skokie, Ill.;
BJ Jones, Artistic Director; Timothy J. Evans, Executive Director.
Presented by arrangement with Robert A. Freedman Dramatic Agency.

Scenic Designer	**Scott Bradley†**
Costume Designer	**Lorraine Venberg**
Lighting Designer	**Brian J. Lilienthal**
Sound Designer	**Matt Callahan**
Properties Designer	**Doc Manning**
Wig/Makeup Designer	**Heather Fleming**
Stage Manager	**Kathy Preher***
Dialect Coach	**Rocco Dal Vera**
Fight Director	**Drew Fracher**
Dramaturg	**Adrien-Alice Hansel**
Casting	**Lynn Baber**

Production underwritten by Todd Lowe and Fran Ratterman.

*Member of Actors' Equity Association, the union of professional actors and stage managers of the United States.
†Designers that are represented by United Scenic Artists, Local USA 829 of the IATSE.

CHARACTERS

CARL ZELAYA, 35, Mexican-American. Lifelong resident of Fronteras. A border patrolman for the past year.

ZELDA PRESTON, 35, Anglo-American. Originally from Fronteras, she left her father's farm at sixteen, returning only for sporadic visits in the intervening years. At the beginning of the play, it has been about 20 years since the farm was her home. She is of Fronteras, but also a stranger there.

ANGIE (OCHOA) ZELAYA, 34, Mexican-American. Married to Carl, she is a lifelong Fronteras resident. She works the underground economy, cutting hair, cleaning houses, and selling home-made foods.

COOPER ("COOP") DANIELS, early 60s, Anglo-American. Lifelong Fronteras resident. A commercial pecan grower and the local spokesperson for the civilian border defense organization Citizens Alliance.

CHUY GALLEGOS, mid-50s. Born in Mexico, he came to the U.S. as a very young man. An expert on pecan farming, he has served as the Preston farm's foreman more than thirty years.

INES (OCHOA) SANDOVAL, 21, Mexican-american. Lifelong Fronteras resident and Angie's younger sister. Six months pregnant, she lives alone in a trailer on the outskirts of Fronteras. Her husband of two years, Georgie, is stationed in Iraq.

TIME AND PLACE

The present. On and around the U.S.-Mexico border in southern New Mexico.

ACT ONE

(In the darkness, the sound of soft guitar music layered with whispering in Spanish. No individual words are discernible. The music fades and the whispering continues for a few moments before it too begins to fade. Finally there is a soft, sustained "Shhh," and then silence as a light rises on Border Patrolman **CARL ZELAYA,** *alone in moonlight, listening.)*

CARL. Most of the time, especially on night patrol, I come up behind them. Real quiet. Not that it matters cuz if they been out there for a few days on foot, they're pretty much cooked through. Blisters all over their feet, their lips. Sometimes their eyes are swollen shut. They don't know or care where they're at anymore, and I walk right up to them. Most times they're out of water, they got no food. Half the time they just sitting out in the open. They got on the wrong shoes – specially the older ladies in their plastic slip-ons or their church shoes, they break your heart, *ese.* They don't hardly blink when I tell them not to move. First thing I do, always, I give them water. And they take it like from a friend.

(He straps on night-vision goggles and scans the horizon as the light on him fades and soft guitar begins to play again in the darkness. Slowly the New Mexico night comes alive with stars. The soft tinkling of wind chimes and the steady chirp of crickets. Dimly visible are the skeletal shapes of pecan trees on the horizon. Lights find **ZELL PRESTON** *standing next to a suitcase, gazing up at the sky. She inhales deeply, enjoying the quiet. The sudden melancholy howl of coyotes in the distance. A moment later, a rooster crows raucously from the darkness*

nearby. **ZELL** *jerks around trying to locate the source of the noise. She pulls a cell phone from her purse, squints at it, and dials. A phone rings as another light rises on* **ANGIE ZELAYA** *checking her caller I.D. She turns the phone on but says nothing. Beat.)*

ZELL. …Hello?…*Hello!?…*

ANGIE. Yeah. Hello.

ZELL. Oh. I'm sorry…Who is this?

ANGIE. Who's *this?*

ZELL. It's Zell Preston. I'm calling for Carlos Zelaya?

ANGIE. I thought that was you. This is Angie.

ZELL. Angie…Angie Ochoa?

ANGIE. Angie *Zelaya.*

ZELL. Oh, jeez, that's right, I'm sorry. Listen, are you at Carlos's – I mean, you're *home*, right?

ANGIE. Yeah. You called here, remember?

ZELL. Right. Well. I'm out here at my dad's. And Chuy was supposed to be here.

ANGIE. He'll be by.

ZELL. Uh-huh. Is Carlos home by any chance?

ANGIE. No.

ZELL. Because apparently they changed the locks at some point? So I'm kind of stuck. You know?…Angie?… Hello-o-o.

ANGIE. I'm still here.

ZELL. Carlos used to have keys to the house out here. Does he by any chance have the new keys?

ANGIE. Nope…I do though.

ZELL. You do? You have keys? Why?

ANGIE. You really wanna know? I clean over there sometimes.

ZELL. Oh. Well. That's great! So can you – ? Um…Is it OK if I come over and *get* the keys?

ANGIE. Why don't I just come over there.

ZELL. That would be *fantastic.*

ANGIE. OK. I'll be there in about an hour.

ZELL. Ohhhh…can you possibly make it sooner? I wouldn't put you out but I've been driving for fourteen hours, and I slept so badly last night at this awful *Marriott* in deepest Oklahoma so I'm a little frazzled and I –

ANGIE. I can be there in an hour, OK?

ZELL. Ohhh-kay. I guess I can just…I'll wait for you here.

ANGIE. *Bueno. Entonces nos vemos.*

(**ANGIE** *hangs up.* **ZELL** *closes her phone and chuckles, deeply irritated. Then she takes a deep cleansing breath and looks up at the stars again. The rooster crows as the light on* **ZELL** *fades and gets brighter on* **ANGIE.** **CARL** *enters wearing his uniform.*)

CARL. Hey.

(*He kisses her.*)

ANGIE. Whoo. You need a shower.

CARL. We got any beer?

ANGIE. How many you had so far?

CARL. Just one. With the guys.

ANGIE. You stink like the *pinche* Bucket.

CARL. You got a nose like a narc dog.

(*He sniffs her closely. She laughs, slaps at him, and they kiss again.*)

ANGIE. Hey, before I forget. Your girlfriend's here.

CARL. Over to the farm?

ANGIE. *Sí, hombre.* Hasn't changed a bit either.

CARL. She's over there right now?

ANGIE. Yeah. That's what I'm telling you, Carl. One beer my ass. She can't get in the house cuz Chuy's not there and she don't got the new keys.

CARL. So what'd you tell her?

ANGIE. Said I'd get 'em to her a little bit later on.

CARL. Why'n'cha go now? You're not doing nothing. Take you ten minutes…Forget it. I'll go.

ANGIE. Chuy don't want you over there.

CARL. Good thing I don't take orders from Chuy.

ANGIE. Look at you, wagging your little tail.

CARL. You come along too, I don't mind. *Pues,* why you gotta make her wait?

ANGIE. Shoulda heard her goin' on about her rough night at the Marriott! Ay, poor thing. Was the sauna broke? Or didn't room service put enough *dulcecitos* on her pillow?

CARL. Just gimme the keys.

(*She holds the keys away. He grabs her and kisses her. Laughing, she pushes him away playfully, puts the keys behind her back.*)

ANGIE. Why you wanna go over there? Tell her you still dream about eating her out?

CARL. *Grosera,* you better not kiss my mother with that dirty mouth.

(*He snatches the keys from her and dodges away, laughing.*)

ANGIE. *Ay, cabrón!*

(**CARL** *exits as lights cross to* **COOP DANIELS** *standing in the glow of a circle of flashlights.*)

COOP. "*E Pluribus Unum.* Out of Many, One." These words are part of the pledge of our great nation, a nation of immigrants. But the federal government is failing here, folks. Failing to end the flood of illegal trafficking across this border. You all know that; it's why you're out here tonight. But remember this: Citizens Alliance is not about playing cowboy. We're here to assist the Border Patrol so they can maybe start getting the job done *right.* Stay calm, stay quiet, and stay with your group. Keep your eyes and ears open, and get on those cell phones as soon as you spot anything at all. Questions?…All right, good deal. Thanks, folks. Let's get to work.

(He turns off his flashlight. The lights cross to ZELL, *sitting on her suitcase. A rooster crows again, loudly. We again begin to hear whispering in the darkness.* ZELL *rises and looks around. She digs in her purse for her phone. The whispering begins to fade.* CARL *appears. Still disoriented and staring intently out at the trees,* ZELL *doesn't notice him until he is quite close to her.)*

CARL. *Hola, guerita.*

*(*ZELL *shrieks, wheels around.)*

ZELL. *Váyate, pendejo! Tengo pistola!*

CARL. Whoa, whoa, whoa! Zell! It's me, it's Carl!

ZELL. Carl...?!

CARL. I brought you the keys! Damn, girl, don't shoot!

ZELL. Oh...Carlos? Oh Jesus Christ, I'm sorry! My God. It is *crazy* out here. Coyotes and barnyard noises and God knows what all – !

CARL. Hey, hey, it's OK now, you're all right, you're OK.

(They take each other in for a moment and then hug a bit awkwardly.)

You almost made me crap my pants just now. You really got a gun?

ZELL. Course not.

(He picks up her suitcase and they enter a cramped kitchen. She gazes around the room. Then, very softly...)

My God...I'm here. I'm really *here.*

CARL. I know, time warp, right?

ZELL. Except for us. Jeez, dude, you got old.

CARL. Not you though. You look great.

ZELL. Do I, ya big liar?

CARL. Yeah. Course you do.

ZELL. Just for that I'm gonna have to see if there's a *cervezita* in here for you. You still drink, right?

CARL. *Pues, ¿cómo no?*

(CARL sits and ZELL opens the fridge and comes back with two beers. She hands one to CARL, who pulls a dollar from his pocket and puts it on the table.)

ZELL. What's that?

CARL. For the beer.

ZELL. Jesus. Don't worry about it.

CARL. It's Chuy's beer.

ZELL. I'll take care of this round.

(She gazes at him for a moment, taking in the full effect of his uniform. He looks right back at her.)

Border Patrol, Carlos.

CARL. Nobody calls me Carlos anymore.

ZELL. *"La migra."*

CARL. *Sí,* Zeldita. Be a year next month.

ZELL. Good lord...How do you like it?

CARL. It's all right. Too many of them and not enough of us, that's all.

ZELL. And when you say "them" you're referring to...?

CARL. Hours are long, but I don't mind. Even if I did, it's my job.

ZELL. You got a pair of those mirror sunglasses?

CARL. Actually I prefer to work at night. It's beautiful out there in the desert, you know. Quiet. The land. The sky. Clear nights, moon turns everything magic...You don't need to be looking at me like that.

ZELL. Like what? I'm not your judge.

CARL. That's right, you're not.

ZELL. I understand: You're making the world safe for democracy.

CARL. Look, I'm not the bad guy, OK? I'm trying to make things *better.*

ZELL. Whoa.

CARL. One time when I was still in training in Arizona we found four of them, OK? Three ladies, one man, but he was really just a kid, you know, couldn't've been more sixteen years old. They were out there in the desert all laying together in a row. Like they were sleeping, camping out. Kid had a note pinned to his shirt. Wrote it with a purple pencil. Told who they were – their names, where they came from. And also the name of the coyote who took their money and left them out there to die, OK? Juan Pedro Escoveda from Jalisco told them a truck would come for them.

ZELL. I was *teasing* you.

CARL. I think about that kid out there, getting broiled alive. And then I think of Juan Pedro from Jalisco. Still in business. Still eating, drinking. Kissing his mother. Going to mass on Sundays –

ZELL. All right. I got it.

CARL. You got no idea. Six weeks back, on a highway stake-out we go to pull over this truck heading north up I-25? Driver slams on his brakes in the middle of the road, jumps out and runs. Five illegals jump out the back… right into oncoming traffic. Three of them dead at the scene. And just recently there was this older lady –

ZELL. Could you…*not* tell another really depressing story right now?

CARL. Oh…Right. Zell, I am so damn sorry about your dad.

ZELL. Well, and since we're on the subject, my mom died too. Last fall.

CARL. I heard that. Damn, girl. That's gotta be a real lonely feeling.

(ZELL nods. Beat.)

ZELL. So. People around here treat you different now?

CARL. You find out who your friends are.

ZELL. Yeah? Who are they?

(They both chuckle.)

Where's your gun?

CARL. Back at the house.

ZELL. Ever shot an illegal?

CARL. Nope. I never shot nobody.

ZELL. But you would if you had to.

CARL. If I had to? Yeah.

(A silence; finally with studied nonchalance...)

ZELL. How was the funeral?

CARL. Aw, you know, it was really something. People came from all over. More than four hundred all together. Saw people I ain't seen since you and me were kids. Line out Avenida Central all the way down to the plaza.

(ZELL nods and turns away from him, breaking down a bit.)

Aww, hey. Hey...We *tried* to reach you.

(He pats her arm softly. She takes his hand and holds onto it.)

ZELL. I know. I know you did.

CARL. *(gently extricating himself)* Chuy told Angie you went on some kind of a...?

ZELL. Silent retreat.

CARL. Right. Right. A "silent retreat." What does that even mean?

ZELL. It means I went out in the woods to meditate and literally didn't speak a word for twenty days and twenty-one nights.

CARL. What for?

ZELL. To clear my head.

CARL. *(chuckling)* Did it work?

ZELL. Yes. Is that funny? *(beat)* OK fine, I could only stand it for seventeen days before I ran out of there screaming.

(CARL shakes his head, chuckles again.)

Anyway. When I got back to my voice mail I found out that on day five of my retreat, my dad had died. And exactly one week later, the good people of Fronteras buried him –

CARL. We couldn't *locate* you –

ZELL. So now I think maybe I need another retreat.

CARL. Or maybe you just need to talk about it…Anyways, it was an awesome funeral and I'm sorry you missed it.

ZELL. My God. He's really gone. Isn't he?

CARL. Yeah. He is. Just fell over one morning out there in the grove.

ZELL. He always said that's how he wanted to go…How's Chuy taking it?

CARL. Me and Chuy don't really talk that much these days.

ZELL. How come?

(CARL gestures to his uniform.)

Ahh.

CARL. What you gonna do about the farm?

ZELL. Trying to get rid of me already?

CARL. Coop Daniels still got a jones for it, ya know.

ZELL. I'm sure he does. Nothing he likes more than sucking up the smaller farms in this valley.

CARL. Last time I checked, you got one to sell.

ZELL. Maybe.

(CARL laughs.)

CARL. Oh, what? You gonna be a *farmer* now?

ZELL. I don't know. I'm kind of in a transition at the moment.

CARL. Silent retreats. Transitions. Man, you like some kinda guru or something.

ZELL. That's me. Oh, and I got fired too. Well. "Asked to resign."

CARL. No way. What happened?

ZELL. I'm not really sure. It was last fall, actually, just about a month after my mom passed…I was getting ready for work one morning and I just…I'd been feeling so… *disconnected*, I guess…it's hard to describe…like I'd forgotten something…or no…more like I'd *lost* something really important but for so long that I'd probably

never be able to get it back...do you know what I...?...
Anyway, that morning, I don't know, this feeling of
being *adrift*...it was so present...I started shaking...and
I just couldn't seem to stop.

CARL. They fired you for that?

ZELL. No, no. I...well. It's actually pretty funny.

CARL. Doesn't sound too funny so far, Zeldita.

ZELL. See, I was part of this team for a new pharmaceuti-
cal product, and we had a presentation scheduled that
morning. The client was coming in, it was this huge
deal, and I was a mess, but I knew I had to be there.
So I drag myself in...and the presentation *starts*...and
it's all fine at first but pretty soon there starts to be this
gap where *I'm* supposed to be...because that's how it
works, you know, everybody's got a very specific *thing
they do* – so my team is looking at me, *waiting* for me,
and the clients are starting to shift around in their
chairs and check their watches, and it's all getting
pretty *dire* and...oh. Did I mention the *product*? It was
this cream especially formulated to shrink and tighten
the tissues of the *vagina* –

CARL. I don't needa hear that –

ZELL. So there I am, everything is spinning wildly out of
control – and yet it's *also* starting to seem a little bit,
um, hilarious? – but I mean, we're about to lose this
account and it's gonna be *totally* my fault – so what
do I do? Well. Right there on the spot, I give 'em a
limerick.

CARL. ...Like...those dirty poems from when we were kids?

ZELL. It popped into my head all of sudden – everything
was *so tense*, ya know? – I just went on instinct: "There
once was a gal from Salinas / Whose twat was too loose
for a penis..." ...Oh, *shit.* I had the whole thing, and
now I can't do it.

CARL. And *then* they fired you.

ZELL. They asked me to resign.

CARL. *Así es la vida triste.*

ZELL. You have not changed.

CARL. Oh, I have, though. I've changed.

ZELL. Nope. Whenever you get uncomfortable you still haul out the Spanish. Come on. That was a funny story.

CARL. *Sí tu dices.* To me it's pretty sad.

ZELL. *(getting two more beers)* Whoo. Tough crowd…Well. You're probably right.

(**CARL** *slaps another dollar on the table.* **CHUY GALLEGOS** *enters.*)

Chuy…*Hey.*

CHUY. *Hola,* Zeldita.

ZELL. Oh my God, I am so glad to see you.

CARL. Hey, Chuy.

CHUY. *Officer* Zelaya.

CARL. I should get going.

ZELL. OK. But we'll talk, right? I'll call you?

CARL. Yeah, do that.

(**ZELL** *kisses* **CARL** *briefly on the mouth, which discomfits him a bit.*)

Oh. OK. Yeah. G'night now…Later days, Chu'.

CHUY. You not gonna check the grove before you go?

CARL. Why? Something out there I should know about?

(**CHUY** *mutters something inaudible.*)

I'm off duty anyways.

CHUY. So you wear that get-up just for fun these days.

CARL. *Pues, sí.* I sleep in it. Shower in it. Can't get enough.

(**CHUY** *mutters again as* **CARL** *exits.* **ZELL** *hands the beer to* **CHUY**.)

ZELL. How you holding up?

CHUY. *Así nada mas,* Zelda. Been kind of a shitty month, you know.

ZELL. Yeah. For me too…

(**CHUY** *looks at the beer bottles, pockets the bills on the table. Outside, the rooster crows suddenly, elaborately.*)

OK, what is the deal with that rooster?

CHUY. El Rey? Aww, he lives down by the Garzas farm but he struts around here like he owns the damn place. Great old fighter, that one, real champ once he gets his spurs on. Twenty-three fights and counting – and he don't just survive, *ése* – he triumphs.

ZELL. I can't believe the state hasn't banned that.

CHUY. They did. But it didn't take.

ZELL. It's barbaric.

(**CHUY** *mutters something.*)

Háblame, Chuy hombre.

CHUY. I said. Tradition matters down here.

ZELL. Throw two birds in a ring with razors on their feet and let them tear each other to pieces. There's a tradition worth hanging on to.

(**CHUY** *gives her a look.*)

What?…Are you mad at me?

CHUY. Mad. No. I'm not mad.

ZELL. But you've got *feelings.*

CHUY. Not gonna deny a few feelings, *jefa.*

ZELL. Don't be an idiot. I'm not your *jefa.*

CHUY. Oh, you're not? I mean *sí, claro*, I worked this place thirty-two years. But fair's fair when there's a legal paper to prove it. And here you are.

ZELL. Well. I'm glad you're not mad.

CHUY. So now you're here, what you planning to do?

ZELL. I'm not sure yet…Are you expecting an answer right this second?

CHUY. Just wondering how long I got before you unload this piece of ground.

ZELL. "Unload it." That's a little harsh, isn't it? I love this place too, you know.

CHUY. Couldn't prove that by the time you spent here these last years.

ZELL. I know it's been a while –

CHUY. A long while.

ZELL. Well, I'm here now.

(beat)

Chuy. I don't blame you for feeling invaded. But you and I have always been friends, and I don't want that to stop...I really need to just *be* here right now. I need the quiet.

*(Beat. **CHUY** finally nods. The rooster crows raucously very near the door and they both jump. **ZELL** laughs and even **CHUY** smiles a little. Then from under the table, he picks up a large box packed with papers and sets it in front of **ZELL**.)*

CHUY. These are your bills.

ZELL. Oh, whoa... Tomorrow for all *that*, I think... Ya know, I heard a lot of action out there in the grove tonight. You got people staying out back?

CHUY. Nah. We don't do that here no more.

ZELL. You're kidding me. Wow. End of an era.

CHUY. Things are a lot tougher now.

ZELL. They used to come right up and tap on the windows during dinner. And they never went away empty-handed. Camped out all over this place. I used to love that. The music at night, the laughing, singing...

CHUY. It's not like that no more. One year *la pinche migra* came by here thirty-three times to check the outbuildings, the far grove, even the back bedroom one time. Your dad, well, he finally just got tired. After a while, *migra* didn't have to bother stop by here no more. They knew they broke him.

ZELL. What about you? They break you too?

(**CHUY** *mutters something.*)

So Dad wasn't hiring *any* labor from the other side?

(**CHUY** *shakes his head.*)

You're telling me he was running this place all by him-self.

CHUY. No, Zelda. We ran it together.

(*gestures to the box on the table*)

I'd look at them bills sooner than later if I was you. I'm gonna turn in.

(**CHUY** *moves to exit.*)

ZELL. You're staying in the big bedroom?

CHUY. …We can switch if you want.

ZELL. That's all right. I just…remember when you used to stay out in the guesthouse, that's all.

CHUY. You mean the *shed.* Been a lot of years since then.

(*He exits.* **ZELL** *looks down at the box of bills, pushes it away. The sound of a Spanish language radio station as the lights cross to* **CARL** *and* **INES***, 21 and six months pregnant, sitting on the steps of* **INES***'s mobile home eating candy bars later the same night.* **INES** *is really savoring the hell out of her candy bar.*)

INES. Mmm. Mmm, *mmmmm*! So what's she like now? Still pretty?

CARL. *Sí, claro.*

INES. Pretty like a movie star?

CARL. I don't know about that. She's messed up like one though.

(**CARL** *yawns.*)

INES. You still all tired, huh?

CARL. I tell ya. Doesn't do me no good to lay down, though. Soon as I do, I'm wide awake.

INES. When's the last time you had a good sleep?

CARL. I don't even remember.

INES. Tía Rosita used to make this herb tea worked really good for that. Less the person got a guilty conscience. Then nothing works...Mmmmm. I could eat twenty of these. More. I could eat a hundred.

CARL. Every once in a while's OK.

INES. Make me fat!

CARL. Well, you gotta eat the good stuff too. Meat and vegetables, protein. I know how you are. You sit around this trailer, get all pitiful, you don't eat. It's not right, Nezzie.

INES. I eat.

CARL. Not enough, *flacita.*

INES. *(rising and sticking her belly out at him) Flacita,* huh?

(CARL rests his hand on her belly for a moment. She laughs suddenly, self-consciously, pulls away from him, looking across the way at another trailer.)

La vieja Truchas. Always at her window. Ay, she's so ignorant. Makes the sign of the cross when she sees me on the street. I keep reminding her I'm *married* but she's old as the dirt, she don't know nothing anymore. She just trailer trash anyways...Ha. Look who's talking, huh?

CARL. Living in a trailer don't make you trash.

(INES is suddenly wobbly and she sits down abruptly.)

INES. Whoo. Got them bright spots in front of my eyes again.

CARL. You tell the doctor about that?

INES. *Pues,* I got my appointment tomorrow.

CARL. You got a problem, you call them up.

INES. Every time I call over there the nurse act like she can't understand me. She's all snotty and everything. Anyways I see them tomorrow.

CARL. Good...Now what you hear from our boy in Iraq?

INES. Aw, Georgie say they just got him digging buncha holes and laying down pipes and stuff. So that's good. And only ten more weeks till he's back with me forever, forever. Whoo, I'll be so big by then! Oh yeah, and he said to tell you you're a *pendejo*. I said I would. *Pendejo*.

CARL. Tell him for me he's a *pinche maricón*...But I mean it, Nez: You gotta eat. Else I'm gonna write and tell him.

INES. *Ay, mentiroso*, you would not.

CARL. If you're having a bad day, don't sit around feeling sorry for yourself. Call somebody up.

INES. Like who? You?

CARL. Yeah. Call me if you need me.

INES. And what? You'll be all like "Oh, hey, um, listen, I got a bunch of Mexicans laying here with their face in the dirt. Can I call you back?"

(*beat*)

Sorry.

CARL. Bring you special treats and look how you do me.

INES. I know. You hate me now?

CARL. *Pues*, I can't stand you. Hey, you want the rest of this one?

INES. You can't finish it? OK then, but I don't wanna get fat, *ese*.

CARL. You're supposed to get fat.

INES. No, just a big belly. I don't wanna get fat for reals. You know how some pregnant ladies get that real wide butt? With those floppy things on the sides? I get like that Georgie won't want me no more.

CARL. Don't talk stupid.

INES. I'm not. *Mira*, he went out with Maricela Ortiz all freshman year and then over the summer she worked at the Dairy Queen and she gained like fifteen pounds. By start of sophomore year, he was all done with her.

CARL. That was high school. Georgie's gonna love you no matter what. You're his wife. You're having his kid.

INES. Yeah, but still…it's a really good thing Maricela got that job at the DQ.

(They laugh. Beat. Then, very quietly)

He's gonna come back, right?

CARL. Sure he is. Damn.

INES. You promise?

CARL. Yes. I promise.

INES. And he'll still be him, right?

CARL. How you mean?

INES. I see all the time on TV how when they come back here, they got all kind a shit wrong with them – health problems, you know, and mental problems too. They come back and they're like mad all the time, they're drinking, doing drugs, or they just lay around in bed all day and look at the wall –

CARL. OK now, Nezzie, just stop.

INES. Tía Rosita gotta come be here with me when I have this baby, that's *it…*

CARL. Not gonna talk about that with you, Nezzie.

INES. It wasn't right what they did to her. She lived here twenty-five years! She paid her taxes and everything!

CARL. She wasn't legal.

INES. She had a card! But somebody broke in her place and stole the Bible where she kept it.

CARL. Come on, you know that's not true. Every time somebody wanna prove a point around here they bring up the *pinche* Bible. She never had a card.

INES. She didn't do nothing. They had no reason.

CARL. They had a reason. She had no card.

INES. Used to be family was more than just some guy and his wife and kids. It was like all these people…you could go in anybody's house and they be happy to see you, they talk to you, listen and joke around with you, give you food, sodas –

CARL. You still got people, Nez.

INES. Family used to be so big…I want that for my baby – I do! – I want him to have more than just me! And now everybody's all the time leaving this place, *always!*… You promise, swear to God, Georgie's coming back?

CARL. Yeah. And you know what else? He's going to be the same old *cabrón* he's always been. Now, if that's what makes you happy, well OK, it's too bad for you but whatever.

INES. *(smiling a little finally and taking his hand)* You got such giant hands. Look at that crazy thing. It's like a oven mitt.

CARL. I gotta go. Here.

(He pulls out a couple of bills.)

Little something for groceries.

INES. I don't want your stupid money.

CARL. Quit being so sassy all the time.

INES. You always giving your money away. Like you so rich.

(But she takes the bills and sticks them in her bra, winking and giggling, then kisses his hand.)

CARL. Señora Truchas is looking.

*(**CARL** tries to pull his hand away; she holds on and continues noisily kissing it. Sound of the rooster crowing in the distance as lights crossfade to the grove. It is early the next morning. Sound of mourning doves and other birds. **CHUY** enters with a wheelbarrow containing a very young pecan tree with a root ball. A coyote yips from a short distance off. **CHUY** pulls a rifle from the wheelbarrow and moves toward the sound, scanning the trees. Seeing nothing, he sets the rifle down and returns to the wheelbarrow. He takes a branch or stub from the wheelbarrow and fits it onto the seedling, then winds the two pieces together with tape to create a single branch. After a moment, **ZELL** enters.)*

ZELL. Hey. I couldn't find the coffee.

*(**CHUY** mutters something.)*

What was that?

CHUY. I don't keep it around. Bothers my gut.

ZELL. Your "gut."…Well. Guess I'll pick some up in town.

CHUY. You'll have to go into Lluvias or up Greeley.

ZELL. Why? Yummy doesn't stock coffee anymore?

CHUY. Yummy been gone couple years now.

ZELL. No way!…Well *shit.*

(She turns to leave, spots the rifle.)

I don't believe it! Is that…?

CHUY. *La Matilda. Sí cómo no.*

(ZELL picks up the gun and points it at the horizon.)

ZELL. Jesus. Dad always loved this rusty old thing.

CHUY. She's not rusty. She can still do her job, don't worry.

ZELL. Since when do you take Matilda out in the grove with you?

CHUY. Family of coyotes up there on the ridge been coming down here for the garbage. And chickens too if they can get them…Hey. It's not a toy.

(ZELL sets the rifle down.)

Something else you need?

ZELL. Nah. Just having a look at the trees…What's wrong with that one?

CHUY. Nothing.

ZELL. Then why are you bandaging it?

CHUY. I'm grafting.

ZELL. What for?

CHUY. Keeps the grove diverse.

ZELL. How does the bandage do that?

(CHUY mutters something.)

I hate to pull rank but that *is* my property.

(She has overstepped and she knows it even before CHUY turns and fixes her with a steady gaze.)

Jeez. I'm *kidding.*

CHUY. I'm grafting a piece of one cultivar onto a seedling of another. This smaller piece is a Choctaw. This seedling here's a burkett, and you know burketts got the best root system of any pecan. I bind them tight like this so they'll go ahead and grow together. Gotta do it in the spring so it has the summer to catch. Then down the road, when this graft bears, you got nuts with the nice traditional Choctaw shape and the better taste of the burkett. Softer shells too...*Entiendes?*

ZELL. *Sí, claro...*I don't remember my dad ever doing that.

CHUY. Didn't use to. But grafting brings a better crop over time. I taught him that.

ZELL. Want some help?

(*Silence.* **ZELL** *gazes around the grove.*)

My dad sort of gave up on me, didn't he?

CHUY. I don't know about that. You were always his baby girl. Maybe he didn't understand why *you* gave up on *him.*

ZELL. I didn't give up on him!

CHUY. Then you should've stayed.

ZELL. I was *sixteen.* What was I supposed to – ?

CHUY. Leaving in the middle of the night –

ZELL. That's a myth and you know it! It was broad daylight! He just didn't get up to say goodbye. *You* did. You got up.

(*beat*)

My mom *needed* me more. He was so...you know how he was.

CHUY. *Sí tú dices.*

ZELL. When we left, he just...built a *different* kind of family. Ya know, I think of all those people who *stayed*...made lives, *families*, right here in Fronteras...He *did* that. He made it all happen. Gave 'em work, got 'em papers, loans. He'd do just about anything for *them.*

(**CHUY** *mutters under his breath.*)

ZELL. *(cont.)* Hey. We used to be buddies. I could always talk to you. Even when I couldn't get through to him. So what the hell happened? Talk to me, Chu'.

(**CHUY** *shakes his head, doesn't answer.*)

Do I owe you money?

CHUY. *Cómo?*

ZELL. I say: Are you owed wages? A salary?

CHUY. End of the week.

ZELL. I have to figure out stuff with the bank, but you'll get your check.

CHUY. Your dad always paid me cash.

ZELL. Fine. And, Chuy, I hope it goes without saying you'll always have a job here.

CHUY. Till you sell, you mean.

(*Sound of car horn. They both squint toward it.*)

A la chingada…

ZELL. Who is it?…Is that Coop? Jesus Christ, what does he want at this hour?

CHUY. What do you think?

COOP. *(off)* Hello there!

(**CHUY** *grabs the rifle, puts it in the wheelbarrow, and takes off in the opposite direction. In a moment* **COOP** *strides on. He is clearly a morning person.*)

Zelda Preston! Mornin', lady! Gosh, it's good to see you. How the heck are ya?

ZELL. I'm all right, Coop. It's been a long time.

COOP. It has, it has. You look great. Did I see Chuy Gallegos skedaddle out of here just now? That guy, I swear, he's like the wind…Zelda. My God. I can't tell you how busted up this valley's been over your dad's passing.

ZELL. Thank you.

COOP. It was quite a funeral.

ZELL. That's what I hear.

COOP. How you doing? Seriously.

ZELL. Well. I'll tell you. If I don't get a decent cup of coffee sometime this morning I'm going to shoot myself in the face.

COOP. Huh. You like French roast?

(**COOP** *reaches into a deep pocket of his jacket and pulls out a thermos. As he pours coffee, the sound of a helicopter in the distance. It slowly draws closer as the scene goes on.*)

ZELL. Oh my God, you're a lifesaver.

COOP. I do what I can.

(**ZELL** *sips coffee as* **COOP** *gazes around the grove. Beat.*)

ZELL. I'm not ready to talk about this farm yet.

COOP. Ha. You get right to the point, don't ya? Just like your dad.

ZELL. I thought I'd save you some time.

COOP. Well, I am interested in this property, that's no secret. But it's not why I'm here. What you up to this morning?

ZELL. Oh…I thought I'd head over to the cemetery.

COOP. I was just there myself.

ZELL. Were you?

COOP. Mmm. I go just about every mornin'…Catherine died, you know. Two years ago now. Cancer. It was… real fast. Relentless, actually.

ZELL. Oh, Coop. I didn't know, I'm so sorry.

COOP. Well. We had thirty-one great years together. But I miss her every day. I do.

(**ZELL** *nods, touches his arm. He chuckles a little, embarrassed. After a moment, he takes a deep breath.*)

Guess I better let ya get on with your morning. But, say, you got any plans later this afternoon, Zelda? Wonder if you'd have time to meet me out by the Wagner place around three o'clock. Got something I'd like to show you.

(They continue to talk but their conversation is drowned out by the sound of the helicopter going past. The lights cross to CARL getting dressed for work. He wears only his uniform pants and shoes. ANGIE enters in a robe. She watches in silence as CARL puts on his shirt and begins to button it.)

CARL. Hey, you.

ANGIE. You still live here or what?

CARL. Couldn't live no place else but witchoo, *amorcita.*

ANGIE. Could've fooled me. I go to bed, you're not home yet. I wake up, you already on your way.

CARL. Nothing been going on in that bed anyhow, so what you care?

ANGIE. That's how it is?

CARL. Lately? That's exactly how it is.

(ANGIE stands very close to him. After a moment, he pulls her to him, kisses her, then nuzzles her neck.)

ANGIE. Hey now, don't start something you can't finish.

(He laughs and they kiss again.)

You thought any more about what I asked you?

CARL. Hmm?

ANGIE. *Mira,* I talked to Tía Rosita on the phone. She says every night she has terrible dreams about Nezzie. You know *mi tía* believes in her dreams but only because most of them come true.

CARL. She can't come back here. You know that.

ANGIE. She's all worried and now she got me worried.

CARL. Once she got deported, that was it. Now I can't do nothing about that, so you gotta stop working me over. Don't put me in a position.

ANGIE. If you coulda heard her. She was really crying.

CARL. She cried all the time when she lived here too.

ANGIE. Her heart is breaking.

CARL. I'm sorry to hear it.

ANGIE. No you're not.

CARL. I love my Rosita. You know that. But she was always crying about something. "The bougainvillea is soooo beautiful"…*(sniffles)* "The Christmas turkey smells so good" *(sniffles and whimpers)* "My friend's sister's boyfriend's uncle got the cancer"…*(sniffles and whimpers copiously)*

ANGIE. That's real nice, Carl.

CARL. "The *mole*, it doesn't taste right…" You know it's true. It's not fair you get her hopes up about this.

ANGIE. *¡No me digas esto! ¡Ella vivió aqui mas de veinte años!*

CARL. Yeah. And then she got swept back down south. Just like a million other people. And that's how it is. That's the world now, OK? You wanna blame me for it, that's your business.

ANGIE. *¡Ay cabrón, tú sabes que la pinche migra no tenía ninguna razón!*

CARL. *¿Yo? Yo no sé nada!*

ANGIE. *(pushing past him)* Excuse me.

CARL. Come on, don't be like that.

ANGIE. This is my family I'm talking about.

CARL. I'm your family too.

ANGIE. Then act like it!

CARL. It's my *job*, God damn it. I notice you like the money it brings in. I'm not gonna have you put me in a position, now that is it.

ANGIE. You and your "position." Wasn't for you, Rosita'd be back over here no problem.

CARL. She gets picked up you really think they gonna believe I don't know nothing about it? In my town? Where I know everybody?

ANGIE. Probably turned her in yourself.

CARL. Hey. You know better than that. If it was up to me, she could come live right here with us. But it's not up to me…Why we gotta fight? I'm so tired, baby. I got a whole big long day looking at me. Can't you just like me once in a while?

(A beat, then **CARL** *moves to put his arms around her again. She pulls away.)*

ANGIE. You overdid the aftershave, *migra.*

*(***ANGIE*** turns to leave.* **CARL** *grabs her and kisses her hard on the mouth. Then he lets her go and they stand there glaring at one another.)*

CARL. Can't keep doing me like this, Angela. I don't wanna fight you all the time.

ANGIE. Then do the right thing, *mi amor.*

CARL. One day you gonna wake up and it's too late. This right here's the family you should be worrying about.

ANGIE. Why don't you go arrest some Mexicans?

(She exits. **CARL** *stares after her then slowly tucks in his shirt and straightens his uniform. The lights cross to* **INES** *kneeling by a grave. She is whispering comfortingly, although there is no one else around. The headstone is small but the area is swamped with flowers, candles, and other tokens. A jointed wooden skeleton is stuck into the ground next to the grave. The sound of a car pulling up and then a door slamming.* **INES** *takes a candy bar out of her pocket, unwraps it, and breaks it in two. She sets one half on top of the headstone and begins to eat the other. After a moment,* **ZELL** *enters, looking around for her father's grave.)*

INES. *Hola,* Zelda. You remember me?

ZELL. …Oh my God…Is that little Ines Ochoa? Of course I do! But look at you! You're all grown up…My God…I remember when you were just a little itty-bitty thing, out there in our orchard picking up windfalls.

INES. Your dad used to give me a penny each one. You come to see him? He's over here by me.

*(***ZELL*** approaches, gazing down at the decorated grave.)*

ZELL. My God, Dad. They forgot the *piñata…*

INES. How you mean?

ZELL. I just meant there's so much…never mind. It doesn't matter. It's lovely.

INES. I know, right? You want me to leave you two alone?

ZELL. No, no, it's all right. Stay…How are your folks, Ines?

INES. Um. That's them right over there.

ZELL. Oh *no*.

INES. Yeah. Car crash. Long time ago now. I don't think about it that much anymore. Ha. Only every day.

ZELL. I know what you mean…I lost my mom a while back too.

INES. Aww. I don't remember her, but I always heard she was a real nice lady.

(**ZELL** *nods, looks away.*)

Getting pretty crowded in here, huh?…Those over there are illegals nobody knew. No IDs, nothing. The church paid to bury them. Pretty soon there's not gonna be no space left for nobody else, you know?

ZELL. Seems like everybody's leaving anyway. Downtown's all boarded up.

INES. Right? Almost nothing left but the diner, the dollar store, and the *pinche* Bucket.

(**INES** *rises and brushes dirt from her knees.*)

ZELL. Oh, wow. I didn't even…Congratulations.

INES. I know, I'm really big, right? You wanna feel?

ZELL. Sure, all right.

(*She does.*)

Wow. Yes, you are. Well, that's really…um…

INES. I'm married.

ZELL. Oh, *good!*

INES. Yeah, to Georgie Sandoval. But he's over in Iraq right now.

ZELL. Ahh jeez.

INES. No, no, he's coming home real soon! Then we have our baby and after that we gonna buy a house maybe up around Cruces and Georgie's gonna go to school and work for his uncle up there doing construction.

ZELL. It's wonderful to have plans, isn't it?

INES. Yeah…You got plans, too?

ZELL. Me? Yes. Yes, I do.

INES. What plans you got?

ZELL. I'm…Well, I mean, who knows? I'm maybe going to…grow pecans…

INES. Yeah? You staying on at your dad's place?

ZELL. Well, he did leave it to me.

INES. You married?

> (ZELL *shakes her head.*)
>
> *¿Por qué no?*

ZELL. I don't really know how to answer that.

INES. *Pues,* won't you be lonely out there?

ZELL. No. I've been on my own a long time, Ines, and I do just fine.

INES. I didn't mean to make you mad.

ZELL. You didn't make me mad.

INES. I'm just sorry for you, that's all.

ZELL. Why?

> (INES *shrugs.*)

I'm fine. I'm so much better now that I'm back here. You have no idea.

INES. Maybe some night you can come eat with me. I got Lean Cuisines or I can fix a pizza.

ZELL. Honestly, you don't need to do that.

INES. It's no problem. I get lonely too.

> (*Beat.* ZELL *finally nods, smiles.*)

ZELL. All right. That sounds nice.

INES. Your dad and Chuy used to come over and eat once in a while. Or sometimes they'd take me out for chicken night at the diner.

ZELL. The diner still does that?

INES. *Sí, claro,* and it's really good too. They give you a *lot*!

ZELL. Man, I used to love chicken night.

INES. It's the best thing *ever*…Hey, you got a car that runs good?

ZELL. Pretty good.

INES. I wonder can I borrow it for a little while.

ZELL. Um…No. Actually, I'm using it.

INES. Oh. OK. That's OK. Maybe some other time.

(**ZELL** *reaches down and picks up the little jointed skeleton.*)

People come every day to bring him things.

ZELL. Just like *Día de los Muertos.*

INES. One day like last week the Correos – you know the ones got the restaurant over by Las Lluvias? – they brought a whole enchilada plate! Beans, rice, salad. Everything! Set it right there on top. I knew it was them because of their red chile. You could smell it all the way from the gate.

ZELL. You come here a lot, huh?

INES. Lotta people to visit.

(*Silence. They stand looking down at the grave for a moment.*)

Everybody here loved him, you know. They never, ever stopped.

(**INES** *touches* **ZELL**'s *arm briefly, then exits.* **ZELL** *stares after her. She then looks down at the grave, notices she is still holding the wooden skeleton. Suddenly overcome, she places it very gently against the gravestone.*)

ZELL. Aw, Dad. Jeez…jeez.

*(But instead of allowing herself to cry, she takes a deep cleansing breath. Then she picks up the candy. After a moment's indecision, she pops it in her mouth. The lights cross to **ANGIE** and **CHUY** in a yard. He is sitting on a wooden chair and wearing a plastic cape. She wears a pocketed beautician's smock from which she pulls a battery-operated hair clipper.)*

ANGIE. It's a damn shame, you know? The old man didn't even like her.

CHUY. *Ay, cabróna,* he loved her, she was his family. Now listen: I *said* a *trim.*

ANGIE. You should lemme do you a favor here, Sasquatch.

CHUY. At least leave me a little on top.

ANGIE. Such a baby.

CHUY. Hey? Last time my sideburns weren't even. One was way up here like this.

(She scoffs and then studies his hair for a moment. She begins to buzz very carefully at the back of his head. She stops periodically to assess her handiwork throughout the following.)

ANGIE. She gonna sell out, you watch. Coop Daniels and her? Made for each other.

CHUY. You still can't get over the fact she used to go out with Carl.

ANGIE. Listen to the wise old *pendejo.*

CHUY. And she found her way outa Fronteras but you still stuck here.

ANGIE. She back now though, isn't she?…Sides, I could get out if I wanted.

CHUY. Not you. This border's got you by the throat.

ANGIE. Nah. I just know one shit-hole's the same as the next. I don't see you packing it up.

CHUY. That's because I love this shit-hole.

ANGIE. Said one turd to the other.

CHUY. I look out the back door, I see my whole life. Right there.

ANGIE. Yeah, sure you do. Only problem is the door don't belong to you. And neither does any of the rest of it.

CHUY. I see the trees I raised. Ground that feeds 'em. And I see all the people who made it happen over the years. Not just me and Press, but your dad and mom too. Tía Rosita. The Zelayas. C'de Bacas. Correos. Most the families in this valley one time or another.

ANGIE. Half them people are dead or deported.

CHUY. Yep. That's what I see. All you see is dollars floating on the ground. Never enough of 'em and blowing all over when you bend down to get them.

ANGIE. *(poking him with the clippers)* Hey. Respect me.

CHUY. I do. But I worry about you too.

ANGIE. Save that for when you get a life.

CHUY. All that bile's gonna choke you one of these days.

ANGIE. You the one with the ulcer, not me. Way I see it, everybody got a choice: You can be a victim or else you can get on with your life.

CHUY. That what you doing, Ange? Getting on with your life?

ANGIE. That's right.

CHUY. You always after the money but you never gonna have enough. Know why? Because anymore you can't even remember why you want it.

ANGIE. *Ah, si?* Carl and me got a house. Two cars. What you got?

CHUY. And it's a waste, too, cuz you're a really smart lady.

ANGIE. *(pulling out a pair of small trimming scissors and beginning to snip)* Smart enough to know I don't like being poor. See, you and me, we can spend our whole life scratching in the dirt. You lived with the old man all these years, took care of his farm for him, what you got to show for that? Now here comes Zeldita, she's lookin' out at them same acres, deciding what she's gonna do with 'em. And you can't say a word about it.

But you know what? When you get your orders to get off her property, you'll be all nice and trimmed up, ready to go.

(Though she is still snipping, **CHUY** *yanks away and rises suddenly, whips off the cape, and turns to face her. They look levelly at one another for a moment.)*

ANGIE. *(cont.)* You see how that is?

*(***ANGIE*** snaps her fingers at him and he hands over his wallet. She plucks out a bill and then hands the wallet back to him.)*

CHUY. So much for scratching in the dirt.

ANGIE. *Sí claro, hombre.* Mama gots to get paid.

*(***CHUY*** jams his hat on his head and exits, as the lights cross to* **ZELL** *and* **COOP** *at the fence. The sound of drilling, pounding, and workers' voices.)*

COOP. Personally? I hate the idea of a border fence, I really do. My family did business with the Mexicans for decades, just like yours did. But get caught hiring them these days you're in a whole world of hurt. So, lookit: we can't *work* them, but they're still coming. Now, a federally funded wall from Texas to the Pacific, that would be great, and it might even happen one day, but until it does, Citizens Alliance is gonna have to go one volunteer project at a time. You look confused.

ZELL. You're building a fence for this rancher, right? But it only blocks off *his* property. So, correct me if I'm wrong, but all an undocumented immigrant's gotta do is head a little east or west to where the fence gives out. So what's the point?

COOP. Well. Last fall this particular rancher was robbed at gunpoint by illegals right here on his own land. Broad daylight. Happily for him, they didn't blow his head off. Next time he might not be so lucky. My opinion, a man shouldn't need that much "luck" on his own ground.

ZELL. Does that happen a lot?

COOP. More often than you think. That's why this movement is funded by donations from thousands of concerned citizens across this region.

ZELL. So what's in it for you?

COOP. I live here.

ZELL. But you've always done pretty well for yourself, haven't you?

COOP. I do all right. But I can't just sit by while illegals gobble up my community's social services and pave the way for the economic free-fall of the industries along this border. Now, I know your dad had his own particular philosophy about things, but this border's changed, Zelda, and ya can't just shut your eyes to that.

ZELL. I'm not.

COOP. Ya see the gal driving the bobcat? She's an out-of-work nurse from Lluvias. Lost her job because her hospital got so overrun with illegals it had to shut down. Third one in the state. These days the nearest hospital is three hours from Fronteras, did you know that? Nearest clinic's sixty-three miles. That gal look like a vigilante to you?

ZELL. No.

COOP. Would you feel the same if she wasn't Latina? You don't have to answer that. But it might surprise you to find out that nearly a quarter of our membership is Latino. See, race doesn't matter to Citizens Alliance – *that* gal, like all of us out here, is simply an American protecting her home against further invasion. Lookit, we're not anti-*immigrant*. We're just a hundred percent anti-*illegal*.

ZELL. No offense, Coop, but I'm just really not much of a joiner, so –

COOP. Did I ask you to join anything?...Here's the deal. Your farm is a conduit and it's been hemorrhaging illegals into this valley for decades. Your dad, God rest his soul, not only let that happen, he encouraged it. Which is why your property's ended up on the Citizens Alliance hot list...And we'd like to fence it for you.

ZELL. I've already got a fence along the back of my far grove.

COOP. That flimsy thing wouldn't keep back a blind two-year-old. I'm talking about twelve feet of high-grade stainless steel along your southern perimeter. For which you won't have to shell out one penny. Now, I know you're not quite ready to talk about the sale of your farm yet, and I understand that, but I'm tellin' you, Zelda, a fence gives that property value-added, no matter what you decide to do with it.

(**ANGIE** *enters with a large box. She whistles sharply to* **COOP**.)

There she is! How many you bring us today, hon'?

ANGIE. Fifty, *jefe.* Just like you ordered.

COOP. So that's fifty at a buck apiece –

ANGIE. Buck-twenty-five, *jefe.* Inflation. Handmade by little old ladies with arthritis in their fingers.

COOP. One thing about you, lady. You don't dicker. Might dick folks around a little bit. But you do not dicker. So fifty times a buck twenty-five…

ANGIE. Sixty-two-fifty.

ZELL. Angie?

ANGIE. *(without turning to look at her)* I was wondering when I'd run into you, *guera.* I see it didn't take you long to hook up with this bunch.

ZELL. Me? No, no, no, I'm not "hooking up" with anybody –

ANGIE. It's OK, don't apologize, you got an investment to protect now, *¿qué no?*

ZELL. It's so not like that.

ANGIE. *(to* **COOP***)* You gonna pay me or what.

COOP. Take a check? Oh, relax, I'm kidding. Don't suppose you could wait a few minutes while I rustle up some cash from my crew, could you?

ANGIE. You should buy them lunch. They're building your wall for you.

COOP. Wall's not for me, Angie. It's for all of us. You included.

ANGIE. Leave me out of it, man.

(COOP chuckles, pulls out his wallet, and counts the money into her hand. She nods and turns to leave.)

COOP. Thanks, lady. Oh, and when you're over on Wednesday, make sure you do the smaller bathroom, OK? I think you skipped it last time.

(ANGIE is gone.)

Gotta love that gal. Real entrepreneur. She's on the go every blessed day mining this border for all it's worth. Bounces around like a pinball, cuttin' hair, cleanin' houses, hawkin' tamales. Bet she doesn't pay a red cent in taxes. You should try one of these things though – they're awful damn good…So. What do you say to my proposition?

ZELL. I'll give it some thought.

COOP. Be a win-win for you. You been back there along the far end of your property line? It's full of garbage. Dirty diapers, spoiled food, God knows what all. It's a hazard. And without a barrier? If you go out there, be real careful, Zelda. I don't want to have to worry about you.

ZELL. I really will think about it. In the meantime, I don't mean to be a jerk, Coop, but I'd really prefer you to stay out of my far grove unless you're invited, okay?

(COOP smiles and shrugs. He hands her a business card.)

COOP. Well now, maybe you don't know this, but I have a financial investment back there.

ZELL. And what might that be?

COOP. I own your well.

(Beat. Then COOP turns and calls off to the unseen workers.)

Who wants one of Mama Zelaya's red hot tamales? Buck-fifty apiece, no waiting.

(He exits. Open-mouthed, ZELL watches him go, starts to follow him, then thinks better of it and strides purposefully off in the opposite direction as lights cross to INES on her steps. ANGIE enters with a small bag of tamales. She hands it to INES and sits next to her.)

ANGIE. Tamales. Eat.

INES. My pressure's up again.

ANGIE. You're kidding me. Why?

INES. Stupid car keeps stalling out. I'm all scared I'll be late for my appointment and I'm all worried and I can feel it starting to go up and then when they put that thing on my arm, it's like my eyes are gonna squirt out my face!

ANGIE. I don't get it. You're skinny.

INES. They said I might have "the clamps" or something.

ANGIE. The clamps? What the hell is that?

INES. It's not good, that's all I know. I don't remember exactly what they said.

ANGIE. What do you remember?

INES. I'm not spoze be on my feet or get excited or drink sodas – *mira*, not even diet! And no salt and –

ANGIE. Did they give you some stuff to read about it?

INES. I forgot it there. They said if things get worse then I might gotta stay in bed till the baby comes.

ANGIE. Because your blood pressure?

INES. I *guess.*

ANGIE. Didn't you ask them anything? Do I have to go with you every single time? You got a question, why don't you ask them?

INES. They talk so fast and they don't listen to me –

ANGIE. That's their job to listen to you!

INES. Plus there's about fifty thousand million people in the waiting room –

ANGIE. You got no idea how to handle *estos putos*. How you gonna take care of a baby, huh? You can't even stick up for yourself. I swear, sometimes I think you're retarded –

INES. I am not!

ANGIE. Wake up! You don't get what you want in this world by crying about it.

INES. You don't get it by screaming all the time either!

ANGIE. Doctors treat you like that because you let them! You don't say a word!

INES. Not everybody's like you, Angie! I need somebody I can talk to! You don't even listen ever!

(**INES** *sits down heavily. She is breathing hard, almost gasping.*)

ANGIE. *(kneeling next to her)* OK, OK, take it easy, Nez. You're right. I'm sorry.

INES. No you're not! Why'n'choo just get out of here and leave me alone!

ANGIE. Come on. Don't say that. I'm glad you're not like me. I'm *glad*. Really. I am.

INES. You can't talk to me like that anymore!

ANGIE. I know. You're right…You wanna hit me? Ándale. Hit me.

(**INES** *punches* **ANGIE** *on the arm.*)

Harder, man. You know you want to.

(**INES** *punches her again. Hard.* **ANGIE** *rubs her arm. Beat.*)

INES. If I tell you something, you promise you won't get mad at me?…I keep on having this dream about Georgie getting blown up. There's pieces of him on the ground and all over the side of his truck and everything.

ANGIE. Everybody needs to stop dreaming so damn much.

INES. And then later, I got the Army letter in my hands, you know – they say if you can see your hands in a dream then it's gonna come true –

ANGIE. Who says that?

INES. – and I could see my hands as plain as day! And then the baby was rotting inside me and falling out one little piece at a time. I found tiny little fingers sticking up out of the carpet all over the trailer and I woke up and my heart was going so fast –

ANGIE. OK, OK, *cálmate, hermanita, cálmate.*

(She strokes **INES**'s *hair gently. Beat.)*

I'm gonna get Tía Rosita back here and she'll take real good care of you, OK? I just gotta figure out how, that's all, but I'm gonna make it happen, I promise. For reals, OK, Nezzie? Come on, don't worry.

(She gives **INES** *a squeeze as the lights cross to late afternoon.* **CARL** *on patrol looking through binoculars. After a moment, he takes out his cell phone, dials.)*

CARL. What you got, Joey?...Yeah, me either. Nothing moving out there...What you think? They getting smarter or we getting dumber? *(laughs)* Little of both. You got that right. Man, it was hot as hell today, right? You wanna go over Correos for a cold one?...OK then. I'll meet you on the ridge in fifteen.

(He hangs up. As he turns to leave, a sound captures his attention, and he freezes. We again hear whispered Spanish, although the individual words aren't discernible. The whispering gets louder but not clearer. In fact, there is a distinctly unreal quality to it that thoroughly spooks **CARL**. *Suddenly there is a sustained "Shhhhhh," and* **CARL** *whirls around, looking this way and that. Silence. He quickly takes out his cell phone again and dials.)*

Mira, you hear that just now?...I thought I...no, it was like talking. Whispering. I don't know...You didn't hear nothing? All right, yeah. I'm just checking. Probably the wires or something...Sunstroke, my ass...Nah, I'm OK. Probably nothing. I'm on my way, bro'.

(He hangs up and turns, scanning the horizon. Still disturbed, he does not holster his gun. The lights cross to the grove. It is near sundown. **CHUY** *is alone looking out at the trees.* **ZELL** *enters.)*

ZELL. Talk to me about the well.

CHUY. What you wanna know?

ZELL. Why Coop Daniels says he owns it.

CHUY. If you look at them papers like I told you –

ZELL. I'm asking you.

CHUY. *Pues...*farm needed a well. Too much drought past couple years. We couldn't count on the ditch running. But your dad didn't have no cash cuz been so long since we had an on-year crop. So he financed it.

ZELL. Through Coop Daniels? I don't believe it.

CHUY. Gotta have water if you gonna grow pecans, baby girl. Daniels gave him a better deal than the bank. *Pinche* vulture. He just hovers and waits.

ZELL. How much do I owe him?

CHUY. Fourteen grand still to go. But you pretty far behind your payments. *Más o menos* seven grand past due right now.

ZELL. That's not that much.

CHUY. It is if you don't got it. And you don't got it 'less you brought it with you.

ZELL. So what can we do about it?

CHUY. You're the boss. You tell me.

ZELL. I know you think I'm completely worthless.

CHUY. I never said that.

ZELL. And you're only staying on here because you love this land and you're loyal as hell and God, Chuy, I can't even tell you how much that means to me. But...I finally feel like I'm *home.* And I just can't see letting anyone take that away from me. I *can't.* I remember who I used to be here. And I *liked* that girl.

CHUY. *Pues sí.* She was a real good kid. But this place ain't like what you remember.

ZELL. Yes it is. It's exactly what I remember. The sky. The air. The quiet. Exactly.

CHUY. You spent too much time in the city. Anything'll look good after that.

ZELL. Just answer me this. If you and I can work the groves the same way you and my dad did...can we make it?

*(**CHUY** looks out at the trees for a long moment.)*

CHUY. Last couple years, me and Press got real quiet, you know? We could go a week without more than a couple words at a time between us. But toward the end of every day, we'd both end up right out here. All day opposite groves, but come dusk, here we'd be. In the far grove. Just a few feet between us and night coming on. Side by side. Like a couple of rock formations.

ZELL. What's it gonna take to keep it going, Chuy *hombre?* Tell me what you need.

CHUY. Press always used to say if you scoop up a handful of the soil from this back grove, you holding a little piece my heart in your hand. It's true too. This ground and me, we belong together. Your dad knew that.

ZELL. You used to eat a mouthful dirt out here every morning. Like vitamins.

CHUY. I still do…You asked me what I want. That's it. I want this grove.

ZELL. Wait. Say that again?

CHUY. And I'm not talking about buying it, Zelda.

ZELL. You want me to just give you the back grove…That's almost half this farm.

CHUY. It's what your dad owed me.

ZELL. Owed you? What do you mean?

CHUY. He knew damn well he couldn't keep this place going without me. When I came here, he didn't know nothing about this land except he bought it cheap from some *pinche cabrón* who already beat the hell out of it.

ZELL. You worked here, Chuy. You got paid.

CHUY. I did. I worked hard. For thirty-two years. He said he'd provide for me. Case he died, said he wanted to make sure I got what's coming to me. Meant a lot to me at the time, you know.

ZELL. Well, I don't know what he meant by that. He never changed his will.

(**CHUY** *nods stonily; beat.*)

So if I agree? What then? What's in it for me?

CHUY. I teach you how to farm this place. I help you hang onto it.

ZELL. My half.

(Silence. Finally...)

How would we do it? What about the well?

CHUY. We make a contract and share the water rights.

ZELL. I meant...Coop wants his money.

CHUY. He'll get it.

ZELL. I've got nothing left of my severance, Chuy.

CHUY. We just need to pay up what's past due and then we'll have a little slack. Once we're caught up we split the well payment every month.

ZELL. Yeah, but how do we get caught up?

(Beat. Finally...)

COOP. Leave it to me.

ZELL. You're sure?

CHUY. Just take me a little time to get things in place. If Daniels don't push us too hard too fast, we be okay.

ZELL. You got a little nest egg put away or something?

CHUY. I said I can do it. That's what you need to know.

ZELL. Right, but I mean what about – ?

CHUY. You're not listening.

ZELL. I'm just trying to be sure about how things –

CHUY. Zeldita. You gonna have to trust me. So. What you say?

*(Beat. **CHUY** solemnly puts out his hand. **ZELL** steps forward, shakes his hand, and then kisses him on the cheek. He is abashed but not entirely displeased. They stand there grinning at each other. The rooster crows mightily as the lights fade.)*

End of Act I

ACT TWO

(About a month later. In the darkness, sustained and ghostly, the indecipherable chorus of whispering in Spanish. Gradually this sound is replaced by music playing very softly. CARL appears alone in light. He gazes out into the darkness for a few moments.)

CARL. I know they're out here. Sometimes I can feel them all around me in the dark. All these eyes looking back at me. So I listen. Wait for a twig to snap. Scuff of a boot on rock. A voice. Sometimes it's so quiet all I hear is my own heart beating in my ears. But I can wait. I got patience. And all the time in the world.

(The lights rise on the desert. It is night. The sound of crickets. There are stars and moonlight. ZELL is sitting on a blanket drinking a beer. There is a partially emptied sixpack next to her. The music is coming from a small old-model boom box.)

ZELL. Jeez, it's like you're at work. Come and sit.

(CARL moves to her, sits on the blanket, pops a beer.)

CARL. So how's it feel being back out here?

ZELL. …Strange.

CARL. Yeah? You don't like the desert no more?

ZELL. I like it.

CARL. But?

ZELL. I just…I mean…

(She reaches over and shuts off the boom box.)

Carlos. What are we doing?

CARL. Just hanging out. Old times, *guera.*

ZELL. Yeah? You tell Angie?

47

CARL. Tell her what? ...We're just hanging out.

ZELL. Yeah. *Here*, though. We only ever came here to drink and fuck.

CARL. Don't say that.

ZELL. What? Fuck?

CARL. I don't like that word.

ZELL. Awww. how many Hail Marys and Our Fathers is it?

CARL. *(chuckling)* Oh, so now you gonna make fun of my faith. You come back to town, you don't hardly call me a month, and now you gonna sit up in here and make fun of me.

ZELL. You could call *me*, ya know.

(beat)

If you want the truth, I'm dead tired by the end of most days.

CARL. I know what *that's* like.

ZELL. I'm passed out by ten just about every night.

CARL. Aww. Just you and Chuy sitting home in front of the fire.

ZELL. Right. I do embroidery while he reads me poetry.

(They laugh.)

CARL. How is ol' Chuy these days?

ZELL. Cranky as ever. But you know what, Carlos? I'm learning so much from him. The work is *endless*. I mean, I *knew*, but I didn't really *know*. You know? Dad never had me do any of the heavy stuff. My *bones* are sore. But I'm getting *muscles*. Feel this. And Chuy's a good teacher. Man, he is so patient.

CARL. So you really gonna do it, huh? You and Chuy gonna split up that farm.

ZELL. All we need is the survey. It's gonna be a couple more weeks before they can get somebody out there. But once that's done it should go pretty quick. And then all we gotta do is pay off the well and we'll be all set, ready for harvest.

(beat)

CARL. Chuy pretty much staying home nights?

ZELL. When he's not out getting hammered at the Bucket.

CARL. I woulda seen him over there.

ZELL. *(chuckling)* Same ol' Carlos.

CARL. You'd tell me if there was something going on, wouldn't you?

ZELL. How do you mean?

CARL. Just asking.

ZELL. What are you asking?

CARL. Chuy keeping his nose clean?

ZELL. Well, okay, off the record? I think he's been going to the fights a lot the past few weeks. The guy always did love a good cockfight, and I know damn well he's betting. It's funny, though: he's got a real soft spot for that monster that hangs around our yard. He brings it little treats, chats away to it when he thinks I can't hear him. It's kind of adorable.

CARL. They crack down hard these days, you know. If there's something going on, you should tell me.

ZELL. Cockfighting's under *migra* jurisdiction now too?

CARL. I'm not talking about that. You just tell Chuy to keep his nose clean.

(She gives him a mock serious nod. Silence for a few beats.)

I miss talking to you.

ZELL. Same here.

CARL. Yeah…Back then…you were like my sister, you know.

ZELL. You fucked your sister?

CARL. There's that word again.

ZELL. Oh, that's right. You don't have a sister.

CARL. I just meant…it was comfortable, you know?

ZELL. I knew what you meant.

CARL. I could always tell you things. And you used to tell me things too.

ZELL. Yeah. Like I told ya you should get the hell outa here and go to college. Damn, Carlos. You wanted to be a vet.

CARL. Can't always have what you want, Zell, or ain't you heard?

ZELL. But you would have been so *great* at it! God, when the Ochoas' dog got run over, you stayed with that poor thing for days. Dribbling water into her mouth with an eyedropper…You were so good with her, so *gentle.* You saved her life.

CARL. Yep. And then some rancher poisoned her like three months later.

ZELL. Carlos, take it from me, there's no point spending your life doing work you hate.

CARL. Easy for you to say. If you get sick of *your* job you just set fire to it and watch it burn. I told you: I don't hate my job. Besides, what else you want me to do? Military? I'd rather keep out an invasion than be part of one, thanks anyways.

ZELL. Come on. Those are not your only options.

CARL. Right, I left out Wal-Mart…*Mira,* your family had money and a good piece of ground, mine didn't. I'm not gonna cry about it, but it's the truth. You took off a long time ago, and you drop by every once in a while just to tell us how we supposed to be living. Me, I stayed right here. I seen my home getting choked, turning into a sewer, and that made me mad.

ZELL. Yeah, you seem mad.

CARL. I'm not mad now. I'm doing something about it. You act like I'm "betraying my people" or something. I'm not betraying nobody. I leave that to the coyotes. Me, I just go to work, do my job, and then go on home. It's not perfect but least I can pay on my house and look my face in the mirror mornings.

ZELL. Does your C.O. know you used to run illegals up north for my dad?

CARL. No, *pues*, I left that off my application.

ZELL. Don't ask, don't tell.

CARL. OK, that's it, let's go.

ZELL. What? What's wrong?

CARL. I wanna talk to my old friend. But all night you just trying to make me small.

ZELL. No I'm not –

CARL. Your dad used to do me like that. Talk like I was too stupid to know he was putting me down –

ZELL. Yeah, well, join the club.

CARL. Always judging me –

ZELL. I'm not judging you!

CARL. The hell you're not.

ZELL. OK, Carl. I'm sorry. I really didn't mean to make you –

CARL. This is where I *live*. You're just down here on vacation from your life. Let's go.

(*ZELL sits down on the blanket.*)

Get up.

ZELL. No.

CARL. You gonna make me leave you out here? Cuz I will.

ZELL. Go ahead.

(*beat*)

CARL. I should do it.

(*But he sits down on the blanket. He gets himself another beer and they sit without looking at each other for a while. Eerie hooting as the coyotes start up in the distance. ZELL shivers.*)

Sounds like they got something.

(*ZELL reaches over and switches on the boom box.*)

CARL. *(cont.)* You have any idea how much shit I gotta eat from people around here? People I grew up with, partied with, they see the uniform and all's I am is *migra*. But you know what, I can't help that. Time for everybody to wake up and live in the real world.

ZELL. Whatever *that* is…I really didn't mean to upset you.

CARL. Got a message for everybody. The good ol' days are gone. And no matter how much you miss 'em, they're not coming back.

ZELL. I know that. I'm sorry.

CARL. All right.

ZELL. I don't know when I'm going over the line with you anymore.

CARL. You never did, *guera, pero no importa.*

ZELL. It *does* matter. Cuz you're my friend and I care about you.

CARL. I know you do. You're just…

ZELL. What?

CARL. "In a transition."

ZELL. No. And I'm not on *vacation* either, Carlos. I live here too.

(Beat. She nudges him. He nudges her back.)

We still friends?

(He finally nods, smiles. They clink bottles and drain their beers. The music on the radio changes to a song they both recognize instantly – it's clearly straight out of their shared past. ZELL laughs and slaps CARL's arm playfully. She rises and begins to dance. She's pretty good too. CARL watches, smiling, and soon he gets up and joins her. They follow each other, each playfully challenging the other to bust a few moves. It is both silly and poignant – a snapshot of their teenage selves.)

You remember this.

CARL. Course I do.

ZELL. Look at you.

CARL. Look at you.

ZELL. You got fat but you still dance pretty good, *moreno*.

CARL. You got kinda stringy but you do OK too, *guera*.

(She laughs, slaps at him again. They continue to dance. After a while, they move closer to each other. They kiss. Suddenly they are surrounded by the beams of a circle of flashlights. CARL yanks away from ZELL instantly, shielding his eyes and brandishing his empty beer bottle.)

¿Quién es? Háblame pues!

(**COOP**, *dressed in dark clothes, appears wielding a heavy-duty flashlight.*)

COOP. Carl? Carl Zelaya, is that you?

CARL. Coop? What the hell you doing?

COOP. You might wanna keep your voice down just a little.

(calling off in a low whisper)

It's OK, guys. Move out. I'll catch up.

(The flashlight beams recede. COOP turns to ZELL and CARL again and just takes them in for a beat or two.)

Sorry to disturb. We heard voices and…well. You know. I was just about to call it in.

CARL. Spoze to notify Border Patrol before you approach a suspect. You know that.

COOP. Probably just as well I didn't in this case, though, huh?

(An uncomfortable beat. ZELL begins to fold up the blanket and COOP turns his flashlight on her.)

Hey, Zelda.

ZELL. Hey.

CARL. Any of your guys out there armed?

COOP. Just pepper spray.

CARL. Mind if I check that out?

COOP. I do mind actually. Since I'm assuming you're not on duty.

ZELL. Come on, Carl. Let's just get out of here.

COOP. Where's your vehicle?

CARL. Up by the road.

COOP. Got a torch?

>   (**CARL** *flips his flashlight on and off.*)

>   OK then. Have a good night.

>   (**CARL** *and* **ZELL** *exit.* **COOP** *watches them go, shaking his head. The lights slowly cross to the grove, early the next morning.* **CHUY** *enters with the wheelbarrow and a seedling with a root ball – it is a bit more filled out than the one in Act I. He takes out a knife and begins to cut into the burlap around the root ball. The rooster crows raucously from nearby.* **CHUY** *smiles and mutters something under his breath in response.* **ANGIE** *enters.*)

ANGIE. Hey.

CHUY. *Buenos.* What brings you out here so early?

ANGIE. You alone?

CHUY. Far as I know.

ANGIE. *¿Dónde está la dueña?*

CHUY. Still sleeping.

ANGIE. You working twenty-four-seven while she's every night out on the town.

CHUY. What town?

>   (*They laugh.*)

ANGIE. How you two getting along?

CHUY. You know me. I get along with everybody.

ANGIE. *(chuckling)* Yeah *right*…Getting late for planting, *¿qué no?*

CHUY. This is the last one right here.

ANGIE. Grove's looking good.

CHUY. I've had help.

ANGIE. Yeah? So she listen to you? She don't give you a lotta shit, try to tell you she know better and all that?

CHUY. Nah. She pays attention. She's catchin' on. And she does real good on the tractor.

ANGIE. Oh, I can see it now.

(Does an unflattering impression. **CHUY** *grins, shrugs. Beat.)*

CHUY. Zeldita's all right.

ANGIE. So you trust her. Well, that's good then.

(beat)

CHUY. So what you need, Angie?

ANGIE. You know Nezzie been sick, right?

CHUY. *Pues sí,* I stopped by to see her yesterday. She says the doctor told her she gotta stay in bed till the baby comes. *Pobrecita,* she's just a kid herself.

ANGIE. Right. Plus her car's broke so I gotta drive her three, four times a week over there to the clinic just to get checked out. She's all nerved up, you know how she gets. Plus it's expensive!

CHUY. She's covered through Georgie, *¿que no?* That's government insurance.

ANGIE. *Sí claro, pero* there's all these "extras" they don't cover. Little shit that adds up real quick. Anyways, Nezzie's a complete wreck. I got some pills could calm her down, but she can't take nothing. And now they talking about putting her in the hospital up in Cruces, which she does *not* wanna do – and I don't blame her cuz you wanna die quick just go stay in a hospital. So now I'm getting really *scared,* you know. Nobody ever lost a baby when Rosita was here.

CHUY. She had a gift, no denying.

ANGIE. She brought Nezzie into this world.

CHUY. I remember.

ANGIE. What you keep in that shed these days?

CHUY. *Nada más* tools.

ANGIE. What if I come fix it up? Give it a coat of paint, put some furniture in there. I could make it real cozy and nice. Only take me a couple days.

CHUY. What for?

ANGIE. Maybe you wanna help me bring over some nice older lady from Mexico to stay in there for cheap.

CHUY. *Estás loca.*

ANGIE. *Migra* don't bother about this place no more.

CHUY. That's cuz I don't give them no *reason.*

ANGIE. It's just till Nezzie has her baby…People come across this border every God damn day.

CHUY. They don't stay in my shed.

ANGIE. "My" shed. Listen to you. You so cute…That guest-house got a long history.

CHUY. You crazy or something? You married to *migra.*

ANGIE. Don't worry about Carl. I can handle him. You gotta do this for me.

CHUY. I don't gotta do a thing.

ANGIE. After the kid is born, Rosita goes right back over. Everybody's happy.

CHUY. *Pues,* I'd like to help you but I can't. Now, you want me to drive Nezzie up Greeley for you sometimes, that I can do, but –

ANGIE. You don't care about Nezzie at all, do you? That poor kid would do anything for you but you just gonna sit by while she –

CHUY. Hey! Don't say nothing you can't take back. Nezzie's my girl and you know that. But I can't risk everything I got. Not now.

ANGIE. What you think you got? Lemme tell you some-thing. You not gonna be laying on your deathbed one day saying "*¡Ay lástima!* I didn't work hard enough on Zelda's farm." Hell, no – you know what you gonna be saying? "*¡Idiota, yo!* I didn't take care of my *gente,* and I hated myself the next twenty years."

CHUY. You give me twenty more years of this, huh? Might interest you to know. That back grove belongs to me now.

(beat)

ANGIE. Might interest you to know I seen you at the Coronado Motel last night.

CHUY. What you talkin' about?

ANGIE. I was taking Nez home from the clinic but just as we're driving outa Greeley she remember she left her purse so we gotta go back. And when I turn my car around, there you are driving along in front of me. Going exactly the speed limit. And I think to myself "*Pues*, what's that *pinche* Chuy up to in Greeley tonight?" And two minutes later, you turn in at the Coronado, drive all the way around the back, and I'm like "Ding! Now I see how it is."

(beat)

You gotta go at least eight miles over the speed limit, don't you know that? Otherwise *migra* come pull you over for sure.

CHUY. There's construction over there.

ANGIE. Don't matter. Speed limit equals *migra*. I used to drive for Preston back in the day, ya know. Only thing: Press didn't take no money from them people. Once they worked enough time here, he just take 'em up north or wherever so they could get on with their life. He was like a good samaritan, *verdad?* You, you're more like...I don't know. What are you like?

*(**CHUY** mutters under his breath.)*

Hey, I'm not your judge. Times change, huh? I understand you *completamente*. Fact I can help you. But you gotta help me too.

CHUY. ...*Háblame pues*.

ANGIE. You do all the driving, they gonna get you. Sooner or later, it's gonna happen. Like I said: I used to do transport for Preston too.

CHUY. I can't have her staying here. Anybody wanders over the border onto our ground, I got nothing to do with it. They on their own.

ANGIE. So? Where you pick 'em up at then?

CHUY. Down there by Los Ruidos. I don't bring 'em noplace near here.

ANGIE. *Bueno. Entonces…*you hook me up with your people. I do some driving for you, we mix it up a little bit. Then one of these days, I go over and pick up Rosita at Ruidos with the rest of 'em. Right? We just gotta find someplace safe where she can stay at.

CHUY. Gonna be tough here in Fronteras. You know how things get around…*Mira,* how about I put you in touch with some people I know up Greeley can find a place for her.

ANGIE. Greeley…Yeah. *Yeah,* that's *perfect.* Nezzie can stay up there with Rosita till she's ready to have that baby. Then she got the clinic *and tía.* I like it! So how soon you can get Rosita over here this side? She's ready to come any day.

ZELL. *(calling from off)* Chuy?

ANGIE. She don't know nothing about it?

CHUY. I got no idea what she knows. This got nothin' to do with her.

(ZELL calls CHUY's name again and ANGIE and CHUY exit together in the opposite direction, as the lights change to later that morning. The sound of a helicopter is heard. INES sits on her steps staring at the label on a bottle of vitamins. Nearly a month has passed since we last saw her, and she is enormous. COOP enters and INES struggles to her feet.)

COOP. No, no, dang, girl, don't get up.

(He helps her sit back down.)

What ya got there?

INES. Pregnant lady vitamins.

COOP. You're getting pretty close now, aren't you? What you got – another month?

INES. Two.

COOP. How you feeling?

INES. …I'm late with your check I know –

COOP. I heard you've been having some cash-flow problems.

INES. *Pues*, I had to quit the diner last month and so now I gotta wait for Georgie's check – but I'm gonna have it should be end of this week –

COOP. How long have we known each other, Ines?

INES. *Pues, no sé...*

COOP. *Pero muchos años, verdad?*

INES. I guess.

COOP. So you gotta know better than to think I'd ever come over here to shake you down for the rent...These trailers are a write-off for me, honey. You know what that means? It means I take a loss on them every single month. I rent them out for not much money to people like you and Georgie. Elena Truchas. The Cabreras. Know why I do that? Because I like to be good to good people. So listen. As of right now, I'm dropping your rent down to one dollar. Now I'm gonna need that dollar every single month. I don't care how you get it to me, but get it to me. All right?...You got a dollar?... Well, hand it over, girl.

(**INES** *pulls out a dollar from her bra and hands it to him.*)

Gracias, eh?

INES. Is this for reals?

COOP. You think I'm playing with you?

INES. How come?

COOP. I told you.

INES. Georgie wouldn't like it. He's proud you know.

COOP. Well, when Georgie's back here where he belongs, we can go back to the old rent and he never needs to know a thing about this. Hell, I'll raise it if that'll make him happy. That work for ya?

(**INES** *nods emphatically.*)

Oh, and I'd appreciate it if you don't mention this to anybody else. I don't want your neighbors feeling like they're getting a raw deal, know what I mean?

INES. *Ah sí, claro!* Thank you, Mr. Daniels, really, OK?

COOP. You ever gonna call me Coop? That's my name... Well. I gotta be gettin' on back to work. You take those vitamins now, ya hear?

(**ANGIE** *enters.*)

Hey, how you doing, lady?

ANGIE. Is there a problem here?

COOP. Not at all. Just visiting with your *hermana.*

INES. He put my rent down to a dollar!

COOP. Now Nezzie, I thought we made a deal.

INES. Oh, shit! I'm sorry!

ANGIE. What's this?

COOP. Nothing. I heard Nezzie had some backed up bills, that's all.

ANGIE. You dropped her rent?

COOP. Is that all right?

ANGIE. It's nice of you.

COOP. I do what I can. We all gotta live here together, ya know. How you doing, Angie?

ANGIE. Well, I wouldn't mind a raise if you're still looking to help people out. Hah.

COOP. *(studying her for a moment)* Everything OK at home?

ANGIE. *¿Mande?*

COOP. You and Carl doing OK?

ANGIE. Why?

COOP. I just...well. With Zelda Preston back in town...I just...I hope that hasn't caused any friction, that's all.

ANGIE. Friction?

COOP. Tension.

ANGIE. I know what the word means. I just don't know why you wanna get in my business.

COOP. I'm sorry. I...I shouldn't have said anything.

ANGIE. You heard something or what?

COOP. I…no, no. Forget it. I…I spoke out of turn. I'll see you ladies around, all right?

(He exits. Beat.)

ANGIE. What he mean by that? You think Carl got something going on with Zelda?

INES. Carl? Nahhhh. You think?

ANGIE. I wouldn't put it past him. Old times, old *putas.*

(She suddenly looks closely at INES.)

What you sweating like that for?…Damn, Nezzie, you look like shit.

INES. I'm not doing so good today. My heart's thumping real hard.

ANGIE. I'm taking you to the clinic. Right now. Get your stuff.

INES. I don't got an appointment.

ANGIE. I don't care, I'm taking you. But hey. Here's something'll make you really happy, OK? I got it all set up. Rosita. She's coming!

INES. …For reals?

ANGIE. Next week or the week after. Just one thing you gotta do for me, OK? You gotta get Carl to quit coming by here all the time. I don't want you two having them big old long talks anymore. You runnin' your mouth gonna be too dangerous for Rosita, you understand me?

INES. I won't run my mouth, I promise.

ANGIE. No, you can't help how you are. So you gotta do this, Nezzie. It's all I'm asking.

INES. What I'm spoze to do when he comes over?

ANGIE. Remember when Jimmy C'de Baca used to come sniffing around after you all the time? How'd you get rid of him?

INES. Georgie kicked his ass back in junior year.

ANGIE. OK, but *before* that you told Jimmy about your boundaries, right? "You can't call me. You can't come by my house. You a nice guy, Jimmy, but you don't need to be coming by." Like that.

INES. Yeah, but Carl's not like Jimmy, though.

ANGIE. I know that. I know. But right now you gotta think of what he does all day and what that means for Rosita, you know what I'm saying? Gonna be hard, but you gotta do this. You promise?...OK then. Get your stuff, we're going to the clinic.

(Music. The lights cross. It is about ten days later. We hear the sound of a crowd roaring, cheering, and two roosters fighting to the death. ZELDA appears suddenly. She is shaking and breathing hard. She hugs herself tightly. The sound of the cockfight crescendos and there is an offstage cheer. CHUY enters. There is a spatter of blood on his face. He holds out a pint of tequila to ZELL. She takes it and gulps.)

CHUY. You wanted to come.

ZELL. I know.

CHUY. Gonna be all right?

ZELL. Uckk, there's *blood* on you...

(He wipes it away.)

Jesus, that was, I mean *Jesus!*

CHUY. You shouldn'ta come.

ZELL. Can we please just go back to the farm now?

CHUY. Not me. I got money on the next fight. El Rey's about to kick some ass in there, you just wait and see.

ZELL. So is *this* how you plan to get the money to pay off the well? By *gambling?*

CHUY. Don't you worry about that. I'm taking care of it.

(He turns to go.)

You coming?

ZELL. I can't go back in there.

CHUY. Nobody forced you to come. Nobody even invited you.

ZELL. I know. I know. I don't know why I came...I guess I was trying to...Did I at least *win?*

CHUY. No.

ZELL. So my guy is…?

(**CHUY** *nods.*)

Jesus. Poor thing.

CHUY. You're not used to it, that's all. Those birds. It's what they live for.

ZELL. That is such a myth! And *my* bird's *dead*! This wasn't my first, you know. My dad took me once when I was a kid. To Palomas. The real deal. Everybody kept talking about "*los gallos valientes*" – like they were heroes or something – these proud fighting birds. And then, just like tonight, the thing starts and I can see they're just panicked, they're scared to death, doing whatever it takes to stay alive another couple seconds. All that jumping and flapping, slicing at each other, people screaming, the smoke. God. When Dad told to sit back down…I threw up. Right there by the pit…He was so disappointed in me. *Again.*

(*Beat.* **CHUY** *nods silently, then pats her shoulder.*)

CHUY. Yeah, your dad, he…sometimes…he just didn't know how to act with you. He didn't mean nothing by it.

(*He hands her the keys.*)

Go on home. Take the truck. I'll get a ride.

ZELL. No, no, I…You sure?

(**CHUY** *nods.*)

You think I'm a big baby, don't you?

CHUY. No.

ZELL. Well, I am. Sometimes I can't imagine what the fuck I'm doing back here.

(**CHUY** *mumbles something inaudible. She sighs.*)

Yeah. OK. Whatever.

CHUY. I said. You're right where you belong.

ZELL. You mean that?

CHUY. Yeah, Zeldita, I mean it. Now go on. I'll see you at home.

(A moment between them. Then a very loud horn sounds signaling the start of the next fight. From off, stomping and clapping. CHUY *turns and exits.* ZELL *stands still a moment, then exits in the other direction as the lights cross to morning at the trailer.* INES *stands on her steps. She is dressed in a robe.* CARL *enters.)*

CARL. Don't you answer your phone anymore?

INES. I'm not really up yet, Carl.

CARL. That's OK…Damn, girl, look at you! You all huge and everything!

INES. I mean I'm not ready for company.

CARL. You mad at me or something?

INES. No.

CARL. You sure?

INES. Yeah I'm sure.

CARL. Then how come you acting like that? And how come you don't call me back when I holler at you?

INES. I got stuff to do sometimes, you know. Things on my mind.

CARL. Can we sit down a second so I can talk to you?

INES. *Pues,* I'm not even dressed.

CARL. That's all right.

(He sits. She remains standing and avoids his eyes.)

Damn, you look even more tired than me. You're all pale and everything. How you doin', Nez?

INES. I wish everybody quit asking me that.

CARL. Seems like you're mad, but I don't know what I did.

INES. Why you wanna come over here all the time anyway?

CARL. What you mean?

INES. You over here all the time.

CARL. I haven't seen you in a week!

INES. Aren't you spoze be at work right now?

CARL. I'm on my way there.

INES. You got so much extra time, maybe you should spend it with your wife.

CARL. Whoa. I just thought I'd stop and see how you doing.

INES. So now you see me. OK?

CARL. Damn, Nezzie, what is up with you?

INES. You come by here like you my boyfriend or something.

CARL. No, like I'm family who cares about you. I really gotta explain this?

INES. *(relenting a bit)* No, but…

CARL. Good. Cuz it would break my heart if you and me stop being family.

INES. If you're cheating on Angie then you're no family of mine, you know that, right?

CARL. *¿Que dices tú?*

INES. You heard me.

CARL. She tell you that?…She knows damn well I'd never cheat on her. She's trying to turn you against me just like the rest of this *pinche* town.

INES. Whatever, Carl. Anyways, you gotta call first.

CARL. I did but you don't pick up the phone.

INES. Well, maybe that should tell you something.

CARL. What's it spoze to tell me? Eh?…*Háblame, hermanita.*

INES. I don't know!

CARL. Angie been talking trash about me. That's not right, Nezzie. You and me always been tight.

INES. You don't need to be coming by here early mornings, late at night, and like that…People talk, you know. People talk around this place!

CARL. This town's always talking. It's a hobby for them. Who cares?

INES. I gotta go back in get my feet up.

CARL. Well, you got a cup of coffee for me in there?

INES. You don't even listen, do you? Leave me alone, Carl! Damn! You always at me.

CARL. *Pues,* if that's really what you want, I can stop coming by.

INES. Just wait to be invited, that's all.

CARL. This is about la Rosita...You and Angie just gonna gang up on me until you get your way, is that it?

INES. Don't blame *mi tía* for this too.

CARL. You sound just like Angie. *Bueno,* Ines. *Ya me voy.* Oh. I almost forgot. Here.

(He pulls a small beany-baby style animal out of his pocket and tosses it at her. It falls at her feet.)

For the baby.

(CARL exits. INES sits down heavily on the step, picks up the toy and puts her face in her hands, as the lights cross to the grove. CHUY enters with a wheelbarrow full of dirt and a shovel. He peers through binoculars out above the treeline. ZELL enters.)

ZELL. I gotta talk to you.

CHUY. That damn coyote's on the ridge again. Just sitting up there with her tongue out. Been watching something down here for the last hour.

ZELL. Hey. I got pulled over by *Migra* on my way home from the fight last night.

CHUY. Oh yeah? What they want?

ZELL. To check the truck. They made me get out, show my ID. And then they took everything out of it.

CHUY. It happens.

ZELL. They tailed me all the way from Tortuga Road before they pulled me over. Something's up. And have you noticed that van out there?

CHUY. Across the road?

ZELL. Two days in a row.

CHUY. Citizens Alliance.

ZELL. Why are they watching the farm? Why now?

CHUY. *Pues,* who knows? Old habits.

ZELL. That's it? You sure about that, Chuy?

(CHUY continues working.)

They can't just *spy* on us. That's harassment.

CHUY. They're not on the property. They just watching to see who comes in and out. They see illegals, they call *Migra*. Got nothing to do with us either way. Don't pay them no attention.

ZELL. Or. Maybe we should think about letting them fence the back grove like they want to.

CHUY. You kidding, right?

ZELL. I'm not. If they're all so worried about what's going on here, let's just show them we got nothing to hide.

CHUY. Your old man would have a fit. We fought that fence ever since they first started talking about it –

ZELL. It's not like we'd be fencing the *border*. Just the back end of *this property*.

CHUY. I said no fence.

ZELL. This is a discussion, Chuy. You don't get to just say no.

CHUY. The far grove is gonna be mine, *¿que no?*

ZELL. You already know it is.

CHUY. Then the fence'd be on my property. And I say no. You forget where I'm from, baby girl. I come a long way since Zacatecas. And I'm not gonna stop anybody doing what I did to get here. Citizens Alliance can spy on this farm as long as they want. Ain't nothing happening on this ground. You got my word on it.

ZELL. ...Okay...But is there anything else you oughta tell me?

(A sharp horn sounds. They both squint off.)

CHUY. *A la chingada. ¡Este cabrón nunca duerme!*

ZELL. What does he want now?

(COOP enters.)

COOP. *Buenos dias,* Zelda. And my God. Is this – ? It can't be! Chuy Gallegos. How are you, sir?

(CHUY mutters.)

ZELL. You ever spend any time at your own farm, Coop? Seems like I see you everywhere else but.

COOP. Well, that's the good news about a big operation. I got people.

CHUY. *Ah sí. Mucha gente. Claro, señor.*

COOP. Whoo, hot today, huh?

ZELL. I'd offer you a soda but we're kinda in the middle of our workday. Was there something you needed?

COOP. Yeah. Yeah, there was. Won't take long, but...it's kind of a private matter.

ZELL. Chuy's my partner. He knows everything that's going on.

COOP. ...All right. I need to talk to you about the well. See, you're coming into this proposition quite a few payments in arrears, Zelda, and I know that's not your fault. Out of respect for your dad, I did allow him to get behind on his payments without taking any legal action. And, boy, I do not want to take any action now either. But...time's marchin' on, you know?

ZELL. It's going to just take us a little while longer to get things back on track here, Coop. I'm doing the best I can.

COOP. I understand. And I think you have to admit I've been pretty patient.

ZELL. Yes you have, Coop, and I so thank you for that.

COOP. But I'm gonna need you to pick up the pace for me a little bit.

ZELL. We're really working on it.

COOP. Good deal. So. How long you figure till you can get current? Just ballpark it for me.

CHUY. *Un mes, nada más.*

ZELL. Oh. Well, I don't know about *that* –

COOP. I can live with a month.

ZELL. I'm not sure we can promise that. But we are expecting a good harvest –

COOP. Oh, I know you are. God willin' and the creek don't rise. Tell you what though. At the moment, my office needs twenty-five hundred dollars of the past-due amount from you as a show of good faith. So I was thinking. If it would help you out to sell your shaker, I'd give you a real decent price for it.

CHUY. Ain't for sale.

ZELL. How much?

COOP. Give ya twenty-eight hundred.

CHUY. It's worth nine thousand.

COOP. *(speaking only to* ZELL*)* Naw. That shaker's more than ten years old. Thirty-five hundred. Apply that to the well and it puts you just about back on track.

CHUY. I said it ain't for sale.

COOP. Zelda?

ZELL. Thanks for the offer, Coop. How about we think it over and let you know?

COOP. Up to you. Just want to give you another option. I try to play fair with my fellow growers.

*(*CHUY *mutters.* COOP *looks at him expressionlessly.)*

ZELL. *Chuy...*We appreciate it, Coop. Really we do. I'll let you know.

COOP. Good deal. And how about this coming Monday for that good-faith payment?

*(*ZELL *looks at* CHUY, *who nods.)*

I'll see you then. Meantime, you behave yourselves now, hear?

*(*COOP *smiles genially and exits.* CHUY *and* ZELL *stand there, staring stonily at one another, until they hear* COOP*'s car start up.)*

CHUY. No way we gonna sell him that shaker.

ZELL. I bet we could get him up to four or five thousand. That gets us a lot closer. Gives us some room to breathe.

CHUY. And what we do about our trees come harvest?

ZELL. We rent a shaker!

CHUY. And you know who you gonna rent from? Besides us, he's the only farm in this valley got a shaker. Now you wanna give him ours too? You thinking like a sharecropper.

ZELL. Don't let your pride lose us this farm, Chuy.

CHUY. It ain't pride. Come harvest, that shaker brings us *income* from the little farms. We make *money* off it… Would your dad have sold his shaker?

ZELL. Who can say?

CHUY. He wouldn't have and you know it. He would have made Daniels come get it. And he'd have been standing by it with Matilda loaded and cocked if he tried it. You gonna fence this ground, you gonna sell Daniels the shaker. Why don't you just hand him over the whole damn thing right now?

ZELL. You told me to leave it all up to you. "Just *trust me*," isn't that what you said? Well, I trusted you. But we don't have the money we owe. So you need to either come up with that money by Monday or I'm selling the shaker for whatever we can get.

(*She exits.* CHUY *stares after her and we hear police radio static and chatter as the lights cross to early evening of the same day.* CARL *is sitting alone in the semi-darkness. He is in uniform but his shirt is unbuttoned and he is drinking a beer. He wears his night-vision goggles.* ANGIE *enters.*)

ANGIE. Halloween come early this year?

(CARL *doesn't answer.*)

OK, so who you spoze to be?…Ahh. The silent treatment. *Bueno* bye.

CARL. What did you say to Nezzie?

ANGIE. Take them damn things off, I didn't say nothing.

CARL. I went over there this morning, she wouldn't even talk to me.

ANGIE. And you found a way to blame this on me. Maybe you should try calling first.

CARL. That's you, always in Nezzie's head, chaca-chaca-chaca-chaca.

ANGIE. I can't help it you go over there, act all weird with her.

CARL. She said you told her I cheated on you.

ANGIE. I never said that.

CARL. I see you, Angie…Even in the dark I see you.

ANGIE. Ohhhhh. Now I get it. That's a good one.

CARL. When you turn family against family, it don't get much wronger than that.

ANGIE. I told you: I didn't say nothing. Anyways, she's not your family, Carl. She's mine.

CARL. Why'd you do it? Just cuz you could? If you hate me that much, why don't you just walk out on me?

ANGIE. You're a stupid, stupid man, you know that? I loved you since I was thirteen years old! But you're changing, Carl, and it scares me.

CARL. I don't know what you're talking about.

ANGIE. Maybe turns out you're not the person Nezzie thought you were. Maybe she's afraid she'll "put you in a position."

CARL. That's you, not Nezzie.

ANGIE. Maybe she don't trust you since you got rid of our *tía*.

CARL. For the last time: I had nothing to do with that.

ANGIE. No? What if it had been my mother? Would you let them take her?

CARL. Your mother's dead.

ANGIE. Would you?

CARL. And she was born on this side.

ANGIE. Would you?

CARL. I'm not playing what-if with you.

ANGIE. What about your mom then?

CARL. Born here.

ANGIE. Would you let them take her?

CARL. This is stupid.

ANGIE. Then it should be easy, *¿que no?* Would you let them send her back, *sí o no?*

CARL. *Bueno*, if she wasn't born here? *Pues*, what could I do?

(Beat; they are both a bit stunned.)

ANGIE. Family my ass. You don't even know who you are.

CARL. I know exactly who *I* am. I'm just not sure who *we* are anymore. How we get like this, baby? Please tell me cuz I don't know.

ANGIE. Oh what, you gonna start crying now?

(ANGIE's cell phone rings. She answers it instantly, keeping her eyes on CARL the entire time.)

Yeah...Yep. I was just leaving. *Claro, hombre, no te preocupes.* I'm on it...*Si, cómo no.* Mm-hm. I got it...*Bueno* bye.

(She hangs up.)

I'm going out.

CARL. Is there somebody else, Angela?

ANGIE. Would that make things easier for you?

CARL. Least I'd know what to do.

ANGIE. Would you, *mi amor?* Without a direct order?

(ANGIE exits. The sound of a helicopter as the lights change to later that evening. CHUY enters the grove with his rifle and a small lantern, and stands scanning the grove, listening intently. The sound of the helicopter increases until its spotlight suddenly catches CHUY, holds on him briefly as he squints up into the glare. Then it moves off once again. CHUY again scans the grove. Suddenly we hear offstage yipping, growling, and the sound of an outraged rooster escalating into a screaming, yowling scuffle. CHUY exits quickly as the offstage battle continues. In a moment, the sound of a rifle blast followed by CHUY cursing in Spanish. ZELL enters the grove on the run.)

ZELL. Chuy?...Chuy, where are you?!...

*(**CHUY** enters carrying a mess of gore and black feathers that was only moments before a large rooster.)*

What are you doing?! What the hell'd you shoot it for?

CHUY. I didn't shoot him. I shot that *pinche* coyote. I grazed her, but she got away.

*(**CHUY** sets the rooster down and kneels next to it, running his fingers gently over its ruined feathers.)*

Ay, El Rey, pobrecito, que hermoso estuvo…

(a brief silence)

ZELL. He belonged to Garzas up the road, right?

CHUY. Aww, yeah, but all this land was his. He was a warrior, *ese gallo.* Lot of heart, you know? Lot of *raza.*

ZELL. I'm really sorry…

CHUY. Twenty-five fights he won. Never a scratch on him. Then along come this coyote decides today's the day. That's all it takes, don't matter what he do.

ZELL. Jeez, I'm so sorry, Chu'…Do you want me to…?

(She motions vaguely at the rooster's corpse.)

CHUY. I don't know what you gonna do. I'm gonna go and bury El Rey.

ZELL. Don't you think you better leave that to Garzas?

CHUY. Garzas throws his dead birds in the dump. This one's gonna have some honor.

*(He gently picks up the rooster again, cradling it in his arms, looks down at it for several moments. Finally, to **ZELL**)*

I ask you something?…Why you think your dad didn't leave me that far grove in his will?

ZELL. I really don't know how to answer that, Chuy.

CHUY. He told me he'd provide for me. Told me I'd *earned* it…So I wonder about it, you know? After thirty-two years…You said he made a different kind of family once you and your ma left here. But maybe there's really only one kind of family when it comes down to it. Or maybe I was always just one more ignorant *pendejo* from below the *frontera.*

ZELL. Aww come on, Chuy. You know it wasn't like that.

CHUY. Do I?

ZELL. Besides, I'm going to make things right with you just like we said. The back grove is already yours – the survey's just a formality. You gotta believe me.

CHUY. I do. I believed him too.

ZELL. Chuy…

CHUY. *(the rooster)* I gotta go do this.

> *(There is a sudden sweep of headlights across the grove and the sound of a car pulling in close.* **CHUY** *immediately reaches down and picks up the rifle.)*

COOP. *(off)* Zelda Preston, you out there?

ZELL. *(to* **CHUY***)* What are you *doing*!?

> *(calling off)*

Be right there!…*(whispering harshly)* Put that thing down – are you crazy? – we don't need any more trouble with him.

CHUY. Just get rid of him. Ándale, Zelda. I mean it.

> *(***CHUY** *backs away into the shadows. In a moment,* **COOP** *enters. He has a flashlight and a cell phone. In the distance we begin to hear the faint whine of a siren.)*

COOP. Evening, Zelda.

ZELL. What do you want, Coop?

COOP. Been some trouble out on the highway I just picked it up on the scanner a few minutes ago. Border Patrol pulled over a truck full of illegals. They got three of them but everybody else took off on foot, including the driver.

ZELL. And so?

COOP. There's reason to believe Chuy Gallegos is involved.

ZELL. Oh yeah? Why's that?

COOP. Border Patrol ID'ed his truck.

ZELL. Chuy's been here with me all night.

COOP. You're gonna want to be real careful what you say now, Zelda.

ZELL. *(calling into the grove)* Chuy. Come out here a sec', will you?

COOP. He's here?

(**CHUY** *edges back into the light.*)

You happen to know the whereabouts of your truck this evening, Chuy?

CHUY. Get off my land.

COOP. 'Fraid you're stuck with me till Border Patrol can get here.

CHUY. I said get off my land. I got work to do.

(He turns in the direction of the far grove.)

COOP. I'm gonna have to insist you sit tight.

CHUY. Yeah? How you gonna do that?

(**COOP** *pulls a small handgun from his pocket. He holds it loosely, not quite pointing it.* **CHUY** *shakes his head, laughs scornfully.*)

COOP. I got my people posted along the perimeter and at the top of the road. So I wouldn't try anything if I were you.

ZELL. Chuy? Everything's *okay*, right?

CHUY. Got nothing to do with you.

(The siren is very close now. It winds down as headlights sweep the grove again. **COOP** *turns and flashes his light on and off several times.)*

CARL. *(from off)* Chuy Gallegos!

COOP. It's all right, Carl! I got him back here!

(**CARLOS** *enters preceded by the sound of his police radio, which continues to crackle and chatter under the scene.*)

CHUY. *Ay, migra.* I knew it'd be you.

CARL. Yeah, you know something? I knew it'd be you too. Sooner or later. I knew it…Coop, what the hell you doing? Put that damn thing away before you hurt yourself…Hey. You hear me? Don't make me haul you in. You know I'll do it.

COOP. *(pocketing the gun)* You guys just cannot accept a helping hand, can ya?

ZELL. Will somebody please tell me what's going on?

CARL. I don't know how deep you're in this, Zelda, but I got a bad feeling. So if you're in it, then please, less you say right now, the better.

CHUY. She's not in it.

CARL. Just you, huh?

CHUY. Just me.

CARL. I don't understand you, man.

CHUY. *Claro, hombre.* You never did.

CARL. All those years I looked up to you.

CHUY. You never knew where to look. You're lost right now and you don't even know it.

CARL. Chuy Gallegos, you're under arrest in connection with the illegal trafficking of undocumented immigrants across an international border. You have the right to remain silent and refuse to answer questions. Do you understand? Anything you do say may be used against you in a court of law. Do you understand?...*Do you understand?*

ZELL. Come on, Carlos, *please.* You've got this all wrong.

(**CHUY** *crosses into the shadows and picks up the rooster.*)

COOP. Watch him now!

CARL. (*putting a hand on his gun*) What you got there, man?...OK, I want you to put it down in front of you... real slow.

(**CHUY** *sets the bird down and* **CARL** *and* **COOP** *both shine lights on it.*)

A la chingada, Chuy! What the hell'd you do?

ZELL. It's just a dead rooster! Chuy's been here with *me* the whole night, I swear to God.

CARL. Just stay quiet, OK? *Please.*

(*to* **CHUY**)

You have the right to consult an attorney before speaking to the authorities and to have an attorney present during questioning now or in the future.

ZELL. It's a *mistake*! Can't we all just go up to the house and – ?

CARL. *I said shut up now!* They got video surveillance from the Coronado in Greeley. Are you aware of that?

ZELL. The Coronado? The motel?

CARL. Know what they got on video? Chuy driving in. Illegals getting out. Chuy driving away. They busted the owner this afternoon. You're caught, Chuy. And don't worry. They gonna get your little friend too. He's on foot and he's not gonna get far.

(CARL's radio has been crackling and there has been static and chatter. Suddenly we hear ANGIE's name amid the static. CARL grabs the radio.)

CARL. One six eight, can you repeat last communication? Over.

VOICE-OVER. Three nine seven, Positive ID on driver of 1987 Chevy Blazer, NM license plate F-R-W dash five oh three. Suspect is Angela Zelaya, 34, of Fronteras. Second suspect apprehended, undocumented Mexican female, fifty to sixty-five, unofficially ID'ed as Rosa Alegria Ochoa. Copy?

(beat; static crackles)

Three nine seven. You copy?

CARL. I copy.

(CARL shuts off the radio and the static cuts out.)

ZELL. Carlos…?

CARL. *(advancing on CHUY)* Why would you do that? Why would you get my Angie mixed up in this?

COOP. Carl, take it easy. Let's all just grab a deep breath here, OK?

CARL. You gonna answer me?! It's one thing for you, man. You're all alone, you got nothing to lose. But that's my wife! You understand me, *pendejo*? My wife!

CHUY. She didn't do nothing wrong. All she wanted was her *tía* come back here.

(Sound of a helicopter approaching. All look up and out. CHUY *calmly reaches down again and picks up the rooster.)*

CARL. What you think you're doing?

CHUY. I'm taking an old friend back to my ground. And I'm gonna bury him.

CARL. You're not going anywhere. Put that fucking thing down.

*(*CARL *unholsters his gun.* CHUY *cradles the bird against his chest.)*

CHUY. What, you gonna shoot me now?

ZELL. Oh my God, Carl...it's just *us*! *Please* put that away!

(As she speaks, ZELL *takes a step or two toward* CARL, *and for a brief moment, as he turns toward her, he is pointing the gun at her. This seems to surprise them both. She stops and backs up.)*

CARL. *(turning again to* CHUY*)* Drop that bird and get your hands where I can see them.

CHUY. You got any idea how stupid you sound, *migra?*

*(*CHUY *turns away.)*

CARL. Coop. Take that thing away from him.

*(*COOP *moves toward* CHUY, *who takes a step into the shadows, puts down the rooster, and picks up the rifle. He points it at* COOP, *who stops where he is.)*

Come on, man. You do not want to do that. Put it down. I'm not gonna tell you again. Put it down. Chuy, I'm warning you. Put. It. Down!

COOP. Give me the gun, Chuy. Come on now.

CHUY. *Lo siento, señor, pero esto no puedo hacer.*

ZELL. Chuy for God's sake! Give it to him!

*(*CHUY *turns briefly to* ZELL *and as he does so,* COOP *takes another quick step toward* CHUY *and gets a hand on the rifle.* CHUY *struggles to regain control of it.)*

CARL. God damn you, stop where you are! *Stop! STOP!*

(ZELDA rushes to CARL and puts a hand on his arm in a final attempt to defuse the situation. CHUY lurches and stumbles a bit, and the gun swings wildly. CARL, distracted by Zelda and seeing CHUY's weapon in motion, panics and fires. The shot hits CHUY in the chest. CHUY lets go of the gun and staggers, staring wildly around the grove.)

CHUY. Oh…OK…Déjame pues. Está bien, está bien, está bien. OK…

(CHUY sits down suddenly, heavily, spreads his hands over his chest and then holds them out staring at the blood with a kind of fascination. The helicopter moves in suddenly; the sound is deafening and the light blinding. COOP signals up at it wildly as ZELL runs to Chuy and crouches next to him. Then, stricken, she turns to CARL who stares fixedly up into the light. The sound of the helicopter slows down and gradually fades to a reverberated thump that is as rhythmic and distorted as the beating of a heart. Finally the beating stops, the searchlight dissipates to black. A short silence then guitar music, as, slowly, lights rise on the grove.)

(It is a bright, clear morning two months later, late summer. For a moment the only sounds are wind chimes and bird calls. CARL enters dressed in jeans and a T-shirt. He gazes around the grove, eventually making his way to the spot where Chuy died. When he's sure he is alone, he kneels and solemnly places a hand on the earth. He takes a small brightly painted wooden cross from his pocket and places it on the ground. Then he begins to pray quietly. ZELL enters with the wheelbarrow full of fertilizer. She stops when she sees CARL. After a moment, she sets down the wheelbarrow and crosses to him, puts a hand gently on his shoulder. He lets out a sharp cry of surprise, rising instantly and moving away from her.)

CARL. Buenas tardes, Zelda.

ZELL. I've been worried about you. I called you a hundred times. Well. You know that…I'm glad you're here.

CARL. I had to see this place one last time.

(*beat*)

ZELL. You going somewhere?

(**CARL** *looks away and says nothing.* **ZELL** *waits a moment, then turns and crosses to the wheelbarrow and, using a coffee can, begins to scoop the fertilizer out and sprinkle it around the base of one of the trees.*)

The day after the funeral, Jimmy C' de Baca showed up at my door. He brought *mole* enchiladas his mother had made for me. He broke down crying when he saw Chuy's hat still lying there on the kitchen table. And he's been back every day since then to help me with the irrigation...He and his dad worked here every single harvest. Big Jimmy and Little Jimmy, remember? Chuy always called them "Los dos Jimmies."

CARL. ...I remember.

ZELL. I sold Jimmy the far grove three weeks ago. Paid off the well... I wanted that land to go to someone who'd worked it. Someone who knows it's special –

CARL. Zelda. You forgive me, don't you? Please. Please, tell me you do.

ZELL. Oh sweetie...

CARL. I can't stop seeing Chuy laying on the ground there...I knew him my whole life. I took this whole place and smashed it. And that one second cost me everything I ever loved in this world. Chuy. Angie. Nezzie...It was an *accident*...

ZELL. I *know* that, Carlos, *I* know. I was *part* of it. I live with that too. I'm up all night sometimes, trying to make sense of it.

CARL. I go up Greeley to see Angie every day but it's so hard to talk in that place. She's so tiny in there. The look on her face breaks my heart. I drive on home and I talk to her all night long in my head. I got no idea what's gonna happen to her. She don't even got a trial date yet.

ZELL. All you can do is keep going up there.

CARL. I can't. I can't do her no good, and it's killing me...I'm leaving Fronteras, Zeldita. I won't be coming back.

(beat)

ZELL. Ya know, just about every day someone stops by here and leaves a little token. I come back from the grove, and I'll find a piece of cake on the porch. Or a bunch of onions, a little carved animal, a note with a blessing. People come and check on me at odd times of the day. Bug me to go to church. I can't quit this place. I'm a part of something here. Even after everything that's happened. And you are too.

CARL. No. Not me. There's nothing left for me here.

ZELL. You're wrong. You've still got people who *need* you. And I don't mean just Angie. Why haven't you gone to see Nezzie?

*(**CARL** doesn't answer.)*

You gotta to go see her.

CARL. She don't wanna see me. I'm poison, and she knows that.

ZELL. Nezzie needs her family now more than ever. She *loves* you. Go see her.

CARL. If I could change it I would. But there's *nothing* I can do.

ZELL. It's not like you to give up without even trying. Please, Carlos. I'll go with you, if you need me to.

CARL. I *can't.*

(silence)

ZELL. There was this chaplain up at the hospital in Cruces where Nezzie delivered. I guess he's kind of an amateur photographer...And if a baby is...when a baby doesn't make it, he'll offer to take some photos of the mother and child together before...you know...So. Nezzie's always going to have a way to remember her little boy…He was so beautiful, Carlos, he truly was. So little. But perfect, you know…That chaplain, that *stranger*, did a small, good thing that meant the whole world to her. You'll want to see those pictures.

(**CARL** *covers his face with his hands.*)

I know you think everything's been taken away from you, but, Carlos, if we don't all take care of each other, we won't have any chance at all.

(**CARL** *finally turns to her. For several moments the only sounds are birdcalls. Then, slowly, we once again become aware of ghostly whispered Spanish rising from all sides. No individual words are discernible. It begins quietly enough but it continues to rise until it gradually takes over the space.* **CARL** *and* **ZELDA** *listen. The lights slowly fade.*)

End of Play

ABOUT THE AUTHOR

LISA DILLMAN's plays include *Detail of a Larger Work, Flung, Half of Plenty, The Walls, Rock Shore, Six Postcards, No Such Thing, Shady Meadows,* and *Ground.* Her work has been produced by Steppenwolf Theatre Company, Actors Theatre of Louisville, American Theatre Company, Rogue Machine Theatre, Summer Play Festival, Hypothetical Theatre Company, and Rivendell Theatre Ensemble. Her plays have been developed by the Goodman Theatre, Victory Gardens, the O'Neill Playwrights Conference, Northlight Theatre, Huntington Theatre Company, Ensemble Studio Theatre, The Women's Project, Philadelphia Theatre Company, the Chicago Humanities Festival, Next Theatre Company, and the National New Play Network. Her short works have been seen at New York's Estrogenius Festival, Australia's Short & Sweet Festival, New Jersey Rep, Theatre Lumina, Collaboraction Sketchbook, and Chicago's Estrogen Fest and Rhino Fest. She has received new-play commissions from the Goodman Theatre, where she was a 2010-2011 member of the Playwrights Unit; Steppenwolf Theatre; Northlight Theatre; Rivendell Theatre Ensemble; the Chicago Humanities Festival; and Imagination Theatre Company. She has received two playwriting fellowships from the Illinois Arts Council, as well as a Sprenger-Lang New History Play Prize (for *Rock Shore*), the Sarett National Playwright Award (for *No Such Thing* [formerly *Separate Rooms*]), and a Julie Harris–Beverly Hills Theatre Guild Award (for *Terre Haute*). *Flung* and *The Walls* were both nominated for Chicago's Joseph Jefferson Award for Best New Play.

Based in Chicago, Dillman is an ensemble member at Rivendell Theatre Ensemble and an artistic associate with Route 66 Theatre Company. She has been a fellow at Blue Mountain Center, Ragdale, and the Millay Colony; a playwright in residence at the William Inge Center for the Arts, Chicago Dramatists, and Western Michigan University; and an instructor at the Victory Gardens Training Center, Chicago Dramatists, Prague Summer Program/Charles University, and the Chicago Public Schools. Her work is published by Samuel French and Dramatic Publishing Company and anthologized in collections from Heinemann, Playscripts Inc., Smith & Kraus, and New Issues Press.

CPSIA information can be obtained at www.ICGtesting.com
Printed in the USA
BVOW11s2030040216

435333BV00009B/81/P